Don't f*ck up your baby
Coen Luijten & Joris van Dooren

Translation: Emma Laboyrie

BIS Publishers
Borneostraat 80-A
1094 CP Amsterdam
The Netherlands
T +31 (0)20 515 02 30
bis@bispublishers.com
www.bispublishers.com

ISBN 978 90 6369 642 9

TABLE OF CONTENTS

MANY, MANY
CONGRATULATIONS!

You are going to build your own brand! Enjoy the moment. As writers of this book, we don't have a clue what your product or service is, but that doesn't matter. If you want to take the first step in building a successful business and launching your own brand, we are here to help you. This book was written to ensure you and your startup have an interesting journey.

Of course, you could still be a little unsure. We can imagine that you are somewhat hesitant because you have no idea what to expect as you launch your own brand. In that case this book will be of great use to you.

Maybe you don't want to start your own brand, but instead you have been tasked with helping someone to transform their idea into a brand. If that's the case, congratulations are also in order.

Congratulations are always flattering, but let's be honest, they don't really help you to succeed. And you can use some help, as a lot of startups fizzle out and die an ugly death. A lot of startup products and services never really get off the ground. What's the reason? Did the brains behind it have

i

a bad idea? Sometimes, but often that is not the case. In many cases, it's a good idea that has cost its initiator a lot of time and energy. In the end, however, they must throw in the towel. They have gained an experience but lost a dream. What a shame.

We don't know what your startup idea is. But if it's a good idea, we don't want you to feel like you've ruined it. You will never have that feeling if you are certain that you've done everything to succeed. That you have taken the right steps, but it has failed, nonetheless. This can always happen. But if you've done everything to succeed, you will be able to come to terms with it.

To fully develop a startup idea is a multifaceted process. Creating a strong brand is an important aspect of that process. We know which steps you must take to transform your startup idea into a new, potent brand. We would like to share these steps with you. We'd love to explain them, so you know what they are for, and how you can navigate them.

That's why we have written this book for you. For you and all others who will someday come up with a startup idea and want to transform it into a real brand.

This is a book for people with a startup idea and who have the ambition to really turn it into a success. But what exactly is a startup? There are several answers to this question. Some specialists, who take up an orthodox interpretation, state that only people who have the ambition to transform their startup into a big enterprise should be allowed to call themselves a startup. "No startup without a scale-up" is their mantra. In this book we take a less dogmatic approach.

The following applies to this book. Startup ideas can be big or small. They can be idealistic or commercial. Or both. Or political. They can be products, concepts, services. They can be simple and practical or complicated and theoretical. The initiator can have the ambition to grow his or her business to epic proportions, or nothing like that in any way. Not everyone strives to create a multinational. A successful one-man business or a company on top of your day job could be just as great a dream.

You're a startup to us if you want to launch your own business. It doesn't matter whether you envision having 1 or 1,000 employees. In the end, good startup ideas have one thing in common: they make people's lives a little or a whole lot better. That's what counts. And that is why they are worth developing.

i

The book you're reading now starts off on the premise that you have a startup idea and sense that you must position your idea well from the very start. It will be interesting for you to see how you can transform your idea into a fully-grown brand. You could view this book as a manual, teaching you how to raise your newborn brand.

A parenting manual?

Let's take a look at what that entails.

It's our day job to teach people how to build up strong brands. As lecturers at Fontys University of Applied Sciences in Tilburg, the Netherlands, we constantly assist students in helping startups become a successful brand. We give lectures and coach the branding process. As a result, we see a lot of startup ideas transform into startup brands.

What grabs our attention each time, and you will probably recognise this, is that startup ideas give the creator an enormous energy boost. We see starting entrepreneurs who combine two full-time jobs. One for a stupid boss and a second full-time job on the side for their own startup idea, all without getting burned out. Quite the opposite, in fact, they have never felt so good. Even though they are investing their savings and are about to part ways with a generous pension plan.

Apparently, when you have a startup idea something happens deep inside your brain, in a part with a difficult name. Don't get us wrong, we don't pretend to be neurologists, but we can imagine a hormonal shot of some sorts that allows you to take on the whole world. A euphoric feeling even. The energy that reminds us of... the energy that parents of newborn babies can have. Young parents and people with a startup idea have the same surprising energy. Do you have a startup idea? Then you have just become a parent!

Congratulations again!

i

A STARTUP BRAND
IS LIKE A BABY!

There are a lot of similarities between babies and startup ideas. Just like babies, startup ideas can give you sleepless nights. They both need to grow. They both demand a lot of your attention. You are prepared to spend a lot of time and resources on them, oftentimes without having a real idea of their potential. You can give them a nice name. You can be blinded by your love for them. For babies as well as startup ideas you can feel and experience a great sense of responsibility. They can give you great feelings of pride, but they can also drive you mad. They teach you a lot about yourself. Their development also makes you go through stages of growth. They can unleash an enormous protective urge in you. If they are in danger, you could be driven to acts you didn't think possible. They can even be more important than yourself.

The most important similarity is as follows: standing at your baby's crib or looking over your startup baby, your biggest wish for them is a successful future.

But what exactly is a successful future? Parents of a newborn have very different views on the matter.

One may hope that their child wins the Olympic gold that for them was far out of reach. Another might hope for a career as a lawyer, scientist or surgeon. Others may have a less defined hope. They hope that their baby can be meaningful for others and as such make the world a little bit better one way or another. While others have less high expectations of their baby. If their baby feels happy both now and later in life, then that's fine.

The same logic applies to startups. One person might want to take over the world with their startup, while another might want to make the world a little bit better. Some startup ideas are interesting for the whole world, others are a small improvement for a select group of people. One startup might envision a multinational headquarter in a skyscraper, while another starter with an idea may just want to experience daily work satisfaction, but would find it unthinkable to have people working for them (and good for them ن).

In other words: success means different things to different people. But what you see as success is not the most important thing. Neither for babies, nor for your startup. What's important is that you realise that success is always a social matter. Success is all about maintaining good relationships with people.

We haven't filled a couple of pages with the analogy between babies and startup ideas just for fun. We're not such big lovers of children anyway. Certainly not Coen, who is childless. And Joris may have three (he denies he has more), but in all honesty, he is happy that they have grown out of their diaper phase. Frankly, we'd much rather work on baby ideas and brands than with real babies. But the whole baby palaver was necessary as an introduction. No worries, we are now getting to the essence of the analogy.

Let's first take a look at how essential the need to be able to build up pleasant relationships is for people and then how this is similar for newborn brands.

Of course, happy recluses exist, but they're a rarity. People are innately social beings. We only function well when we can connect with our fellow people. People need to have friends and only grow in their career when they can work together with others. Good relationships lead to a co-working structure which helps us forward and lets us grow. Bad relationships lead to conflicts, which generally don't benefit anyone.

Babies parents know this, whether consciously or unconsciously. A large part of upbringing, therefore, boils down to how you should relate to others. Fathers and mothers try to raise their child in such a manner that they are able to build relationships with other people. That's why they teach them that biting another toddler is not done. That playing nicely together is a lot more fun than punching and kicking your playmate. That it's OK for another child to briefly play with your toy car. That telling the truth is better than lying, because otherwise people won't be able to trust you.

All in all, parents put a lot of effort into ensuring their baby grows up to be a good person that others like to be around.

The future happiness of a baby depends on the degree to which it can build relationships with others. It's about connecting with other people. And the interesting thing is that this works the same with startup ideas.

A STARTUP DOESN'T
SELL ITSELF

Your startup's success also depends on its relationship with all kinds of people. This is not just about clients who see its value and want to buy it. You need business partners. And suppliers. Investors maybe. Or how about your own social environment? Often you need their support. These are all people. People that must connect with your startup idea. Feel sympathy for your idea. Or even better, identify themselves with your idea.

Wouldn't it be great if those people could find you and your startup idea effortlessly? Maybe that's what you're hoping for. As the saying goes, a good idea sells itself. Sadly, this is bullsh*t. We're not saying it does never happen, but as Austin Kleon puts it in his book **Steal like an artist:** "If your ideas are any good, you will have to ram them down people's throat." Good startup ideas don't sell themselves. People are seldom open to them.

This is why. In a sense, our world looks like an enormous supermarket. A French Carrefour, for example. If you happen to go to France, go into a shop like that and try picking a dessert. Or a Walmart in America will also do. Have you got any idea how many different desserts they have? We don't know the exact number, but at 243 we stopped counting. And we weren't even halfway then. We only know now that it's a shocking number. The same applies to a lot of other products. The aisle of biscuits? Enough for the rest of your life. Breakfast cereals? It's crazy how many different types of breakfast cereals you can choose from and how similar their packaging looks. It's no longer a sea of options, more like a tsunami which you are bound to drown in. It leads to shoppers suffering from choice overload. They solve this by blocking out a lot of the information that is fired at them.

The annoying part is: a lot of products and services can, to some degree, be compared with desserts, biscuits or breakfast cereals in the supermarket. There are a lot of them and they are all fighting for people's attention. So it's hard for your startup idea to stand out in the cluttered ocean of brands. Even if your startup idea is pretty unique.

To summarize, this is the challenge that you face when you have a startup idea that you want to expand. On the one side you have a sea of ideas. On the other side you have the people you need for the idea to become successful. They will need to maintain a relationship with one another. The big question is how they will find each other as all these people don't have enough time to delve into the enormous number of ideas floating around.

i

That's why we believe that you should help these people. We can do this by kneading the idea until it becomes fine relationship material, just like parents do with their baby. You will succeed when you are able to transform your startup idea into one of their favourite brands. How you do that is the focus of this book. Therefore, you can view this book, like we said earlier, as a parenting manual for newborn brands.

Of course, a lot more is required than just a strong brand to successfully launch a new business. Here as well, the same analogy with young parents applies. An adorable baby is lying in its cot and from one moment to the next you're expected to be an expert on babies. The infant forces you, usually through deafening screams, to develop and apply your knowledge with regard to nutrition, hygiene, sleep patterns and medical care. And that's only the beginning. It takes a village to raise a child, right? Well, it takes a village to raise a startup too. As a parent of a newly born startup, you are also expected to be an expert on everything overnight.

From financing, legal matters and taxes, to bookkeeping and in some cases production processes... You will have to deal with a lot of stuff. Unfortunately, we can't help you with all those issues. We don't have sufficient expertise in these fields. Rules also differ widely per country or industry. But there is something that we can help you with: marketing and communication.

Almost everyone understands that a newly launched startup needs to work on its brand visibility. After all, you can't buy what you don't know. Your first reflex will be to immediately fire up your social media. This wouldn't surprise us. Facebook, Instagram, Twitter, Snapchat, TikTok, LinkedIn; all those platforms are very easily accessible. A snap accompanied by an enthusiastic text are placed within minutes.

We strongly advise you to refrain from posting for now. It's not enough to have a sympathetic aunt who is enthusiastic enough to share your post. You need to have a message that resonates with other people. Even hits the spot. Therefore, you should take your time to think about what you really want and what would really do the job. How will your startup idea transform into a popular brand? Or, how do you create such a prime position that people will choose your newborn brand?

Please wait a bit and take the next 18 steps with us, after which, you can go wild and introduce your vulnerable newborn startup idea to the world as a strong, fully-grown brand.

i

A brand is strong when enough people have developed a preference for it. The question is how to achieve this. Of course, in the past a lot has been done to try to ascertain how people choose and develop their preferences. Many scientists have delved into this matter. For a long time, it was thought that people were very calculating when developing their preferences and making choices.

However, we aren't rational beings at all. We are, as Dan Ariely puts it in his fittingly titled book, **Predictably Irrational**. Our decisions aren't the result of carefully weighed pros and cons. It's an impenetrable process. Scientific attempts to study choice processes have yielded valuable insights, but the most important conclusion is that we still don't know very much. The view that we have of the decision process of humans is comparable to a captain's view of an iceberg: he sees its tip, but the 80% that is under water remains out of view.

Naturally, much thought has gone into the bottom of the iceberg. Philip Kotler is someone who has developed interesting thoughts on this subject. He assumes that the decision-making process of an individual is a complex interaction of stimuli that mix with the personal traits of an individual. The puzzling messing around of cortexes, neurons and hormones in the individual's gray mass is fed by a mixture of environmental factors. They can suddenly briefly enter the picture, like the obtrusive wrapper of a candy bar at the till for example. Or they can be a continuous presence in life, like the cultural aspects people grow up with. Think of the serious longing people can have for a mistletoe, every time Christmas comes around.

The price, the economic situation, the analysis of your own needs, social contacts, the character... They can all play a role. The question is which role they play in practice. There isn't really a decisive answer. People can't indicate how exactly the interaction works. Not for somebody else and not for themselves either. The process of developing a preference and making a choice is, as Kotler puts it, a **Black Box**.

Kotler's ideas are worth examining a little further. Let's go back in time 55 years. In 1967 Philip Kotler presented his now world-famous stimulus response model. Pretty ahead of its time. This model was born out of a need which marketers still have in our present time.

Kotler wanted to know what is required of consumers in order for them to buy products or services. He set about to find out the how and why of consumer behaviour. Marketers want nothing more than to know exactly how consumers react to the different marketing activities of businesses. What Kotler wanted to know was how people choose. Super interesting, right? To us it feels a bit like looking for the holy grail and actually finding it... Just imagine.

After a lot of research Kotler came up with his Black Box model. A model should be a simplified version of reality. If Kotler has succeeded in simplifying the reality of purchasing decisions, that reality must have been extremely complex. Even the simplified model seems complex to us, so we've decided not to show it here. Instead, we would like to explain to you the basic premise of his idea in simple language, after which we will show you how to manipulate the Black Box to make a success of your newborn brand.

To understand the model, we ask you to imagine yourself as an average consumer. You are just living your life. Doing your thing. In your life there are numerous companies that want something of you. It could be anything, it doesn't matter what. They send you what Kotler calls stimuli. Put more simply, companies talk to you and want to convince you that it's beneficial to go into business with them.

Companies send you these stimuli via the so-called marketing mix. This mix contains the price, the ad messages, the distribution channels and even the design of the product itself. According to Kotler, other stimuli come from your own environment, such as your political, social, economic and technological environment. In other words, a lot of stimuli are fired at you.

These stimuli, which are also called the external factors, combine forces in your mind. Kotler calls this the buyer's mind. And in your mind some other things are added to the mix. The values you've been brought up with, your self-image, your lifestyle, your interests, the culture that you are part of.

It gets quite busy in the buyer's mind. Somehow all these ingredients communicate with one another. You weigh up the pros and cons, you feel, you rationalise, you ponder, you consider.

This process can unfold slowly or rapidly. Some neuromarketers agree that it happens super-fast. They claim that purchasing decisions are made in a part of the brain that doesn't rely on logical reasoning, but instead, operates on an emotional basis.

If a stimulus triggers the release of dopamine in your brain, you will want the product before you have even thought about it. Logical arguments are used later on, when you justify your purchase to yourself and others. In any case, a decision is rolled out. Kotler calls this the response. And the response is pretty easy. Either you buy the product or service or you don't buy it. Voilà, you've made your choice.

In 1967, Kotler realised that he had come up with an interesting overview of the ingredients needed for the process happening in the buyer's mind, but that he didn't have a clue how the buyer's mind would subsequently operate with these ingredients. That's why he called it the Black Box.

You can imagine that a lot of people find it very interesting to unravel the workings of the Black Box. When you've found out, you can capitalise on it and you are in business. You will know exactly what you should do or say to convince someone to buy your product or service. Or, in this case, to build a relationship with your newborn brand.

Has anyone succeeded in completely unravelling the Black Box? Nope. The holy grail is still nowhere to be found. And even though we are marketers ourselves, we are happy no one has succeeded yet. Imagine, a buyer's button that really works. Scary as hell!

Exciting, the mystery of the Black Box. But we can hear you thinking over: what purpose does this serve for my own idea? Well, a lot in fact, as we aren't completely in the dark when it comes to the ways of the Black Box. Even before Kotler, different fields of science, such as psychology, sociology, philosophy and neurology, fired up little lamps that illuminate the Black Box somewhat, and thus help you forward.

With these insights in mind, you can analyse and tweak your newborn brand to influence people's Black Box. This increases the likelihood of people deciding to connect with your newborn brand.

Put more simply, we are going to help you to develop your startup idea in such a way, that it becomes an attractive new brand, triggering people out of thinking they have to make a choice. They've picked your brand even before they become aware of it.

i

NOW WE ARE WHERE WE ARE SUPPOSED TO BE!

We want people to pick your brand instead of someone else's. The real challenge has become crystal clear. Your baby brand needs to find its way into the mysteriously operating Black Box of the people you need to make your startup idea into a success. And to come out as a winner, let's not forget that part. In order to achieve this, your startup idea needs to be transformed into a fully-grown brand. Let's work on that.

From this point onward we will take a practical approach. We will discover that you can play with specific values, convictions, emotions, and much more. The good thing is that you can shape a developing brand much more than you could and would do raising a child. We are going to play with the DNA, the character and the look of your brand, among others. We will give you a step-by-step manual to help you turn your newborn brand into a grown-up brand. To raise it. To help you strike the right chord in the Black Box .

We have come up with 18 steps. Some of these steps you can easily carry out yourself. The tools, instruments and examples we will give you are meant to really give you a leg up. Having said that, it could be that some steps lead you to the insight that you need help.

In order to establish whether you want to carry these steps out on your own or need help with some of them, you could use the so-called three-hour rule. We were taught this rule by Pim Stuurman, one of the founders of Tweetbeam. He states that a lot of things are less complicated than you initially think. But certainly not everything. In order to discover whether something is within or outside of his reach, Stuurman reserves a three hour slot. In those three hours he reads up on the case and gets down to work. If, at the end of the three hour period, he finds out that a satisfying result is far out of reach, he hires an expert. To us this seems like a smart way of going about it. You could also work this way.

We have another piece of advice. Most people in your network are willing to help. So if, after the allocated three hours, you are in doubt of your own judgement, check your LinkedIn and speak about it with an expert. This is nearly always possible.

Enough talk. We are going to get down to business. On to step 1!

i

DESCRIBE YOUR
STARTUP IDEA

First things first. We've already seen that ideas can come in all shapes and sizes. They can be small and merely relevant to a couple of people. Or they can be enormous, and form the basis for a future multinational. And everything in between, so to speak.

It's good at the start to have a clear picture. Which startup idea are you going to work with? What do you want to turn into a newborn brand? What is it and what is it about? At the start of the journey, it's a good idea to write down a couple of sentences that describe your idea. Don't lose speed. It doesn't have to be perfect just yet. Not at all. Otherwise what would be the point of the rest of this book?

Example? Right. Airbnb.

Yes, nowadays this is a mega company, with a stock market value of almost 25 billion dollars. But Airbnb also started as a startup idea in 2007. After a lot of struggles and rejections this startup idea started growing from 2010 onwards into the established brand it is today.

At the time, the idea of the Airbnb's three founders could be described as follows.

Conferences are regularly being held in San Francisco. As a result, hotels are often fully booked. So, the idea is to rent out our own space with an air bed and breakfast, to make some extra money.

And this is exactly what happened. In 2007 the three founders decided to rent out 3 air beds including breakfast, amounting to a cost of 80 USD per person for three nights.

And now you. Take your first step on the next page. Don't hesitate and start the raising process of your newborn brand. Enjoy the moment!

1

MY STARTUP IDEA IS:

Briefly describe to yourself your startup idea. You should use a maximum of five lines to describe this.

...

STEP 2

CHOOSE YOUR
TARGET GROUP

Your startup idea needs to relate to people. A connection needs to be made. You shouldn't have to raise your voice in order to be heard, which is what a lot of companies do these days. You should instead talk to the right people. If you want people to connect to your idea, it's smart to think about which people you want to reach out to and how you want to do that. Entering into relationships is easier when you have a clear view on your target group. What the heart thinks the tongue speaks, but it's pointless blurting out enthusiastic stories concerning your idea to every Tom, Dick and Harry. It's hard to sell cars to people who want to stay at home.

So, who are the people that suit your idea?

Let's try and paint a clearer picture of the target group for your idea. You can insert this information in a stereotypical sketch of a person. This will then transform into what is called a persona: a detailed description of a fictive person that would be enthused by your idea. You can add as much detail to your persona as you want. You can add all sorts of things to it. Where someone is from. What kind of income he or she earns.

2

Their sex. Age. Level of schooling. Type of employment. Family status. Cultural background. Interests. Lifestyle. Maybe even their political preferences. And also very useful: the type of media your target group likes to use. You can make this overview as concise and detailed as you like. You just add what you think is relevant.

A persona lies at the core of your target group. You should paint a clear picture in order to get a good overview. Don't take it lightly. Investing now means you can reap what you sow later in your trajectory.

As you're getting into detail, you're creating a kind of passport for your persona so to speak. You can add a photo to it. You know the saying; a picture says more than a thousand words. Wait. Let's show you a random example. A filled-out persona passport, just to give you an idea.

We will use the brand Eat Natural for this example. An interesting and growing brand that has been active for 20 years. And what do they do passionately at Eat Natural? They use honest ingredients to make the most delicious breakfast cereals and granola bars. With whole nuts. Soft dried fruit. Wholegrains and seeds. In their own words: our reason for getting out of bed every day is to make (and eat) the best tasting bars and breakfast cereals. Praveen's (one of the founders) goal: eating a snack bar should make you feel happy. You can already sense that a bar like this will appeal to a certain group of people. That there are people who fit this idea.

Let's take a look at how we can translate their idea into a potential persona.

Name: *Siri*

Nationality: *Dutch*

Age: *29 years old*

Sex: *Female*

Living situation: *Single family home in Amsterdam*

Education: *University of applied sciences*

Income: *Twice the average*

Relationship status: *Living together, recently became mother to her first child, so rather busy*

Cultural background: *Typically Dutch, tolerant and open-minded*

Political leanings: *Slightly progressive, slightly centre left, worried about social and environmental issues*

Hobbies: *Running and every now and again fitness*

Interests: *Eating healthily, drinking white wine with friends on the terrace. City trips, but that will become harder now that the little one is here*

Active on: *Facebook and recently more on Instagram*

Is sensitive to: *The opinions of girlfriends*

And now you for your startup idea!

MY PERSONA IS:

Name:

Nationality:

Age:

Sex:

Living situation:

Education:

Income:

Relationship status:

Cultural background:

Political leanings:

Hobbies:

Interests:

Active on:

Is sensitive to:

THE VALUE OF
YOUR STARTUP IDEA

Hopefully you have your target group in focus. They should be the ones opening their Black Boxes to your idea, because they experience the added value of it. That value is a crucial element within the Black Box. It forms the pinnacle of the match between your idea and these people.

The question you should ask yourself is: what can you say about the added value of your idea?

Value is a complicated concept. Let's try and unravel this complexity a bit. An idea is good when it makes the world a little bit better. According to marketers this is the case when your idea fulfills a certain need of a group of people. Sometimes they are aware of this need themselves, other times, they haven't even figured out that they have this apparent need. Did you know you needed an iPhone before it was invented? Apparently only Steve Jobs knew. People don't really know what they want.

The complexity of the added value stems from the fact that it's a concept which is made up of a lot of different layers that link together. Let's make it simple. We will limit ourselves to the two layers we deem the most essential to you. The functional layer and the emotional layer.

The functional layer of your idea is actually pretty simple. It refers to what the idea's user can achieve with it. You should view it this way: the user is up against a challenge and your idea helps them to complete the challenge. Just like the function of a watch is to tell the time. Right? There can be several functions, of course. Most often this will be the case. Red Bull lessens your thirst, but it also keeps you awake. Durex prevents pregnancies as well as STDs.

Beneath the functional layer is a layer that is much more complicated. This is the emotional layer. Choosing to use a product or a service goes hand in hand with a lot of emotions. The choice for a specific car is usually influenced by feelings which a particular model or brand stir up. You can use it to show yourself and the rest of the world who you are and what you represent. And that's something that makes you happy and proud.

The emotion can even be stronger than the function. There are loads of people who drink Red Bull even though they aren't thirsty and don't need to stay awake. Rather, they want to show themselves and the rest of the world that they are pretty tough. And a Rolex, yes, it let's you check the time, but it seems more of a statement of success.

3

The functional layer is important, but the emotional layer is even more important. It forms an important starting point for the rest of this book. Emotions play a part in almost all subsequent steps.

Thus, the emotional layer is very important, but at the same time very complex. Emotions often form a web with one another, they fluctuate, come into your life and are context-bound. Let's take an example in order to explain how this can pan out. We would like to take a look at the functional and emotional layer of a product used worldwide: the bicycle.

Bicycles come in all shapes and sizes. Ranging from the superfast road bikes you could complete the Tour de France with to full suspension downhill mountain bikes on which you can race down a rocky ski slope in the summer.

But most people, of course, aren't thrill-seekers looking for a potentially lethal speed kick. They just want to get from A to B in a town or city. Going food shopping, riding to work, clubs or their studies. For those people you have the city bike. And we're going to take a look at it now. To be precise, we are going to be looking at a model designed by the hip Dutch manufacturer, Vanmoof.

This is it, the Vanmoof S3:

Let's start off by taking a look at the **functional layer**. This layer has to do with the product itself.

The bike was conceived two centuries ago as a product idea. Its basic function hasn't really changed in all those years: transporting yourself and perhaps your backpack or shopping bag from A to B. It's a cheap and easy way to get from your home to work, the sports club or school. The setting has, of course, developed a little bit since then. In the last couple of decennia, we have come to appreciate the sporty and environmentally friendly side of cycling more and more.

Now, we're cautiously getting to the emotional layer of the product. The emotional layer directly links into the functional layer and makes it relevant.

3

Those who cycle feel that they're doing a good job. It makes you fit and is environmentally friendly. Every reason to feel rather pleased with yourself whilst pushing the pedals. All bikes can, of course, give you this feeling. So what makes the Vanmoof S3 feel so special? How have they appealed to the emotive side of cycling in order to achieve an appealing and distinctive market position?

Well, there are also a lot of emotions attached to cycling that are less positive. You are often faced with headwind or a massive hill on your route. You arrive at your destination drenched in sweat. Not so bad if you are on your way to the gym and you can cross the warming up off your list. You'd feel rather awkward on the other hand, if you arrived at your lecture at the university or a business meeting with sweat patches on your underarms after a cycling trip. Even though you can't do much about it, it makes you feel insecure, and you might even feel a bit embarrassed.

Should you take the car or public transport then? Not at all. Bike manufacturers have come up with a solution: the electric bike. It's still a lot more environmentally friendly than the car, especially if you use green energy. The electric motor on this bike effortlessly takes you up to speeds of 25 kms an hour. Even with headwind and going uphill. It allows you to feel good about yourself, without the profuse sweating and panting. Vanmoof's S3 model has a built-in electric motor, but this isn't really any different from its competitors. It's not what makes the S3 special. Vanmoof has achieved the S3's ability to standout by highlighting another emotional function: the worry that your bike might get stolen or vandalised.

Electric bikes are popular but they certainly aren't cheap. You usually have to park your bike in a public space on reaching your destination. And public spaces don't just contain decent citizens. In urban environments especially, it's hard to predict what kind of idiots hang around there. In the blink of an eye, someone could throw your beautiful bike into the back of a van, and ten minutes later put it up for sale on eBay. Or a passing joker tries to impress his friends by kicking in your lights. In other words, you park your bike and double lock it, feeling rather uneasy. Hoping for the best, planning for the worst. Not nice at all.

It's exactly this emotion which Vanmoof has focused on. From their first models onwards, they have integrated their bike lights into the frame. This means that it would take you a whole lot of effort to ruin the lights. Arsehole proof.

With the S3, Vanmoof has done even more to reassure the owner. The bike contains a lock that you can activate and deactivate with your smartphone. This means you're the only one who can use the bike. Theft has become pointless. On top of that, you can use the app to locate your

3

bike. A find my iPhone function for your S3. So, if someone decides to take your bike after all, you can go and collect it yourself. Or if you find this a rather scary idea (which we can well imagine), Vanmoof even has a team of bike hunters at their disposal that can take this risky business off your hands.

Reassured? We would think so! Like no other, Vanmoof has taken the emotional layer that comes with the use of their products seriously. Great work that has won them a lot of fans.

As you can see, a product or service idea revolves around a lot more than merely the functional layer. You need to dig deeper in order to connect with your target audience. The emotional value, that's what it's about, especially in the well-known Black Box.

Do you feel us? Nice that your startup idea is functional, but the real value that forms the foundation on which you can build a relationship lies deeper. You want to create a connection between your idea and your target group.

But how do people connect to something? Truly valuable connections, between people as well as people and ideas, come from a click on an emotional level. You can identify with somebody or a newborn brand, you share the same underlying values and ideals, you inspire each other, you feel mutual respect and you feel truly understood. That is the basis for building a relationship. It's a relationship that transcends the functional reason for choosing an idea.

Now, it's essential for you to get a grip on the functional and emotional layer. The functional layer might not be so hard to map out, but those emotions... Holy fŭck.

Although...You can arrive at the deeper layer by answering just five questions. These are the questions, with the answers provided by us for the Vanmoof S3.

1. What does your target group want to achieve?

Get from A to B in a practical, sporty and environmentally friendly way.

2. Which negative emotions can arise in the process?

The fear that the bike could get stolen or wrecked and the insecurities that this leads to. Wondering whether you might be better off choosing a different mode of transportation.

3. How does your idea ensure that these negative emotions disappear?

Hip, slick, but most importantly, arsehole proof design. Almost impossible to break. A built-in lock that only you can activate and deactivate. An app that lets you

3

*see the location of your bike. A bike hunter service
for the rare occasion you need it.*

4. Which positive emotions does this bring the target
group?

*The feeling that you can even park your bike in a
dodgy area without having to worry. It's all going to
be OK! Peace of mind, Vanmoof writes on its website.*

5. Which positive emotions now have the space to
flourish?

*Joy, because you're being active. And pride, because
you're saving the planet.*

Really. It's that simple. Or maybe not?

This may be harder than you think. These
are tough questions. You need a lot of insight
into people's minds to answer them. In most
cases people aren't able or prepared to tell you
themselves. Understanding your emotions and
talking openly about them: it's not a given for
everyone.

Whether people will tell you that they're really
anxious about vandalism and bike theft when you
ask them about the negative side of biking remains
to be seen. Empathy is essential to get your five
questions answered. Is empathy your thing? Good,
in that case the questions are probably not too
hard for you. But you might find it difficult. In any

case, it's a very good idea to get talking to your future clients. We would like to give you the golden tip for when you strike up the conversation with your target audience. Ask further questions.

The good thing is, there's a simple technique for it. We call it the whywhywhywhywhy technique.

Why? is the best question there is in countless situations. It's open and inviting. It's a good question to frequently ask your manager or your teacher, by the way, but that's another story. When you ask someone about their feelings with regards to a particular challenge or job, ask them at the end of their answer (which will probably be rather superficial): Why? An answer will follow, after which you ask 'Why?' again. If you repeat this five times, you may want to explain at your third 'why' that you are deliberately using a technique, otherwise you might get slapped in the face. It's necessary nonetheless, because after asking the 'why' question five times, you usually arrive at the core of people's emotions. Or at the end of the so-called ladder, because this technique is also referred to as laddering.

Emotions rarely come alone. Are you frustrated? Then you're probably sad and angry too. Are you in awe? This usually comes hand in hand with some fear. Relieved? Then you're probably happy too. So don't pinpoint one emotion, but work with those combined emotions. What if you get

3

a complex web of emotions that shoot off in all directions? Not a problem, we will tackle this later in step 7.

To conclude, we should put things into perspective a bit. That whywhywhywhywhy stuff sounds great, but asking people about their motives may not be the most decisive way of gathering information. If, as neuromarketers claim, decisions are made subconsciously, you're probably best off by adding observation, empathising, or making brain scans to the mix. OK, forget brain scans. Who on earth has a spare brain scanner lying around? Nevertheless, combining different methods is always a good idea.

MY FIVE QUESTIONS AND ANSWERS:

Q: What does my target group want to achieve?
A: ...

Q: Which negative emotions can arise in the process?
A: ...

Q: How does my idea ensure that these negative emotions disappear?
A: ...

Q: Which positive emotions does this bring the target group?
A: ...

Q: Which positive emotions now have the space to flourish?
A: ...

3

LET'S ZOOM OUT
AND REFLECT

Once you've made a serious attempt to unravel the value of your idea and have a clear picture of your target group, take a short break. That's definitely a sensible idea in this process. Maybe you should do it after each step.

Now, the time has come to zoom out and to reflect. Does your startup idea really have value and can you identify it? If so, proceed to this fourth step. If not, you might be better off analysing the whole thing more thoroughly to find out where the functional and emotional values of your idea exactly lie. Or maybe you should head back to the drawing board and fine-tune your startup idea. Or even part ways with your startup idea and come up with a new one. If you are in doubt, we have an interesting additional question for you. As things stand right now, is it the right time to come knocking on the door of the Black Box with my startup idea?

Some people are way ahead of their time, others think they are ahead of their time. We ourselves belong to the latter category, especially on rainy days when we come up with bad ideas that don't catch on. Others are late to the party with their idea.

All the mentioned cases are problematic, because timing is essential. The Black Box's front door resembles that of a private home. You run the risk of being greeted by a moody occupant armed with a baseball bat, should you ring the doorbell at the wrong hour. Or the owners are in such a deep sleep, that the door remains shut.

But how do you know whether it's the right time? Well, you never know for sure until you get down to work. There isn't a clock that can predict such a thing. It's always a bit of a gamble. We can tell you, however, that things get much easier once you have an idea which suits the zeitgeist. Or even better, one that is just ahead of its time. This is the case when an idea fits a certain trend.

Discovering a trend is a matter of looking around you. Which large movements do you see? What are large groups of people suddenly concerned about? And do you think this will be the case for the foreseeable future? In other words, which trends can you spot that connect with your idea?

In his book **Zag**, Marty Neumeier compares piggybacking off a trend, to surfing a wave. If you manage to catch the right wave, you can go at

4

great speeds. Maybe with your idea you'll even be able to do something you can't do surfing: riding multiple waves at the same time. Why would you limit yourself to just one trend? What if you can't spot any trends that match your idea? In that case you're either too late or too early coming up with your idea. In the first instance, no one will know what you're talking about. In the second instance, people will keep smiling at you, but label you as a moron. In both cases, you should think carefully about continuing your journey.

If you've singled out one, two or even more trends, then you're heading in the right direction. Below, we've added three ideas that have benefited from the trends of this century.

> Healthy food, user-friendly culinary discoveries: *Hello Fresh and other meal plans with fresh ingredients.*

> Hip, professional, flashy sustainability in transportation: *Tesla*

> Personalised exercise in a social setting: *Strava*

FITTING TRENDS:

My idea fits the following trends:

...

4

MAPPING OUT
THE COMPETITION

As we've said before, there are tons of products and services. This makes it a challenge to launch a unique or distinguishing startup idea. We've run up against startups that claim they don't have any competition. Bullsh*t. You'll have to deal with competitors anytime, anywhere, so make sure you have spotted them. Before you take the next steps, it makes sense to look at how your neighbour builds his place. Before you know it, you've built exactly the same house.

Competition occurs on different levels. You have direct competitors and competitors that are less obvious. Direct competition comes from the ideas that resemble yours the most. Imagine that you've come up with square peppermints. In that case, round peppermints probably form your direct competition. If factors like the taste and the price are about the same, then it's only the shape that's different. Less direct competition could be chewing gum.

Take a good look around you. Which ideas are logical alternatives to your idea? Which alternatives are obvious? And which ideas are further removed from your idea, but are in the same playing field, nonetheless? Can you notice anything that stands out in the way in which these ideas are presented?

All sorts of things could catch your eye. Certain emotions they try to evoke. Specific colours they use. Promises they make. A striking tone of voice. A rock-solid slogan...

Write it down, map it out. Do it right, but don't spend too much time on it. At the end of the day, you need to rely on your own strength. If you keep looking at your competitors, your heart will sink into your boots. And that's a shame, because it's avoidable. The rest of this book is filled with all the steps you need to arrive at a place that will set you apart.

Let's take an example. You may know the brand Sodastream. It currently operates in 46 countries. What's Sodastream's background story? Sodastream wants to make a difference by making disposable plastic bottles obsolete. With a Sodastream machine you can turn tap water into sparkling water in a jiffy. According to their website that's easy, delicious and sustainable. Are they unique? Nope. They have multiple competitors. Imagine they're just starting with this idea. Then it would be handy to do research into Aarke, Mysoda, ISI and KitchenAid. They offer a similar idea. What catches your attention? Note it down!

5

MY COMPETITION:

Fill out who your direct and indirect competitors are and what stands out.

...

CREATE
UNIQUENESS

You now have a clear picture of what extras your idea offers and to whom. You know who your competitors are and you've decided that the world is ready for the launch of your idea. If that's the case, we recommend you write down all insights you've had regarding your idea, in such a way that the promise of your idea becomes crystal clear to others. You are ready to prepare an onliness statement. This cool concept is another present Marty Neumeier has given to the world. Neumeier has deduced it from the Unique Selling Proposition pioneered by Rosser Reeves in the 1940s in ad campaigns. Reeves always focused his communication campaigns on a distinguishing aspect of a product or service in order to drive sales.

A focus is indeed what it's about. Formulating an onliness statement is a simple way to help you bring focus to your idea to set it apart from other ideas. In order to fill in this model you need to find out what added value your startup idea brings others.

If you succeed in putting it the right way, you have pinpointed the most important part of your startup

51

6

idea's DNA. In one snappy sentence you show what you offer and who you offer it to and what sets you apart from all those other ideas.

Hang on. Here is the model Marty Neumeier had in mind.

My startup idea is:
The only (product or service you offer) ...
that (what makes you unique) ...
for (target group) ...
in (regions of business) ...
who want (need state) ...
in an era of (fitting trend) ...

As you can see it contains 6 different fields you need to fill out. These fields correspond to the steps we've taken up to now.

The only focuses on exactly what you are doing. What is your idea?

That aims at what is special about your idea?

For is concerned with marking out your most essential group of people, whose Black Box you want to enter.

In points to how you wish to mark out your territory. It can be a geographic area, but also an industry, a sector or a corner of the online world. Or maybe even a combination of all those things.

Who want focuses on what the target group wants to achieve.

In an era of refers to the trend that fits your idea. Here you can note down the trend that your idea piggybacks off. In what kind of timeframe are you launching your idea?

Want an example? We'll go back to Vanmoof's S3 electric bike.

The only electric bike that uses arsholeproof design and intelligent protection from theft for cyclists in urban areas all around the world who want to park their bike worry-free in an era in which vandalism and theft sadly pose an actual risk.

You can fill out an onlineness statement for practically every idea. Here is an example for our very own University of Applied Sciences in Tilburg.

The only university in the Netherlands that is completely dedicated to marketing and communications for enthusiastic people with inquisitive minds, who want to build up a future in one of the marketing and communications specialisations and who realise that they need an inspiring network of students, lecturers and business partners in times in which education is seen as a value creating process in which the journey is more important than the destination.

6

Now it's your turn!

MY ONLINESS STATEMENT

Fill out the onliness statement of your startup idea!

The only ...

That ...

For ...

In ...

Who want ...

In an era of ...

CHOOSE YOUR
ARCHETYPE

An idea for everyone is usually an idea for no one. It's a good thing that we've been able to apply some focus. But we are still left with the issue of the emotions that we've mapped out. They often shoot off in all directions. That's a problem as you cannot use your communications to target a different emotion every day. Your target group won't have a clue what's going on. Let's apply some focus to the emotions. We are going to try to channel them. And in order to do so, we are going to introduce you to Freud, Jung and their archetypes.

We've seen that scientists that focus on the behaviour of people have provided relevant insights in the modus operandi of the Black Box. Sigmund Freud was among these scientists. We are definitely a fan of Freud, as he is famous for his Freudian slip, which so ruthlessly tears off the veneer of civilization from your behaviour. During the process of writing this book, we had a lot of sex... uh, setbacks ☺.

Sigmund Freud himself had never heard of the Black Box, but he got the fact that people can't picture what happens inside it like no other. He divided the mind into two different parts, so to speak, that operate more or less independently from one another. The conscious and the subconscious. Together they explain our behaviour and therefore the choices we make.

Of course, it isn't as simple as we are presenting it. Here and there has been ample scientific criticism directed at Freud. Freud, however, seems to say the same as the quoted neuromarketers. It looks like the unconscious takes the centre stage in the Black Box. If you really want to let your idea shine in the Black Box, it's worth trying to get your startup idea to appeal to the unconscious.

Carl Jung, one of Freud's pupils, has found out how you can do this. It's difficult stuff but Jung's approach is elegantly simple. We're fans. We use his insights daily and have known for some time: it really works.

If you google Carl Jung's photo, you mostly get to see charming black and white pictures of an old gentleman. Not exactly how you'd picture a pupil. Briefly scanning his life teaches you that he and Freud disagreed on plenty of things. It's the classic case of a pupil that is on his way to surpassing his master, leading to all sorts of friction. Add living in challenging times, with two World Wars and some accusations of Nazism and antisemitism to the mix, and you wonder: when will the Netflix series premiere?

Anyway, that's not what this is about. The point is that Jung further elaborated on Freud's theories of the subconscious and arrived at the following insight. People's behaviour is influenced by aspirations and driving forces in the unconscious. And an important addition to this, a number of those driving forces and aspirations are found in every human being. They are independent of your culture and your religion, rather, they are universal. Jung called this the collective unconscious.

Males, females, the young and old, according to Jung we all have several identical driving forces. Even though we aren't aware of these, they strongly control our behaviour and choices. Jung called the images, stories and situations that appeal to our universal driving forces, archetypical. These are moments when you come in contact with forces which propel you into a typical behavioural role. Such a behavioural role, is called an archetype.

We can't escape archetypes. Even docile types sometimes have the urge to rebel. The biggest laggards sometimes succumb to the urge to become better at something. The ambition to discover the world is felt by the biggest hermits. The strength of these driving forces and how often we feel they trigger us may define our character.

We believe that you can couple the web of the emotions surrounding your target group to such an archetype. Using your startup idea to consistently play an archetypical role, you invoke the same relevant emotions each time. These emotions give your idea meaning to your target audience. This way you can create deeply anchored connections with each other in the unconscious. A click happens in the Black Box, with people hardly noticing it.

Recognizably and meaningfully entering the Black Box is exactly what you want with your newborn brand. You can do this thanks to archetypes. The choice of an archetype is surprisingly limited. Small disclaimer: there is disagreement on how many archetypes exist, varying from a lot to eight or so. Most experts, however, work with twelve primary archetypes, as did Jung.

We find that working with an archetype is an essential aid to consistently applying focus to the playing field of emotions. These emotions give meaning to the brand. Through them we are able to generate a connection between the brand and the target group. They lend your brand its recognisable character and therefore influence all subsequent steps in this book. The choice of an archetype is a super important step for you. We will try and help you with it the best we can, which means we'll take our time.

Let's start off by looking at which archetypes exist in the first place. Subsequently, we will present twelve successful brands and explain how they use one of the twelve archetypes. We've chosen historic and well-established brands that are famous worldwide. They usually have a multinational company as the driving force behind them. We know this is a little boring and would rather have surprised you with things you didn't even know existed.

However, we have consciously chosen well-known brands. It will help you to feel the essence the accompanying archetype represents and which emotions it evokes. This will help you to realise how important it is to look further than the obvious when you're analysing the value of your newborn brand.

The stories about the brands on the next pages are our own descriptions, based on numerous vague internet sources and stories. Too many and too obscure to list here. We've tried our best not to compromise the truth.

What we do find important to mention though is a crucial source we've used, the Dutch book **De vijf stappen naar een betekenisvol merk** (The five steps to a meaningful brand), by Michel Jansen. It's a very interesting book that you could read (in case you speak Dutch) if you want to learn more about the use of archetypes in communication.

7

We've also added a pitfall to each archetype. Let's hope you don't fall into it.

And yes. People are also critical of the archetypes. They aren't always universal and there are cultures that view things differently. True, it isn't maths, but our experience is that singling out an archetype for your newborn brand really helps in getting focus.

Another small pitfall. You take your startup idea as the starting point from which to determine your archetype, not your own personality and emotions. Even though you're the parent of your startup idea, you yourself aren't your startup idea. You are branding your startup, not yourself.

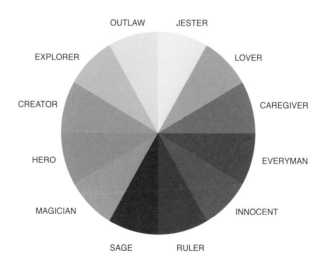

ARCHETYPE
JESTER

Why don't we start off with something that makes us all happy? Ice cream. In 1978, Ben Cohen and Jerry Greenfield thought it would be a good idea to open up an ice cream shop after completing a written course in ice cream making.

Ice cream is not really a product that can solve problems, unless you want to use it to soothe a sore throat. But it is really delicious. You might initially think that you could send it into the Black Box with a message that this is an idea you can enjoy. Ice cream presented as a product to fall in love with. If we look at Ben & Jerry's success, we see that they've focused on other emotions, which has led to the rollout of the Jester archetype.

In the process of determining their value proposition, they must have arrived at the conclusion that ice cream mainly makes life fun. You don't eat ice creams at funerals. (We don't. If you do, though, enjoy). You eat ice cream at times when you want to celebrate life. Buying and eating an ice cream is a moment of fun and joy. Rarely alone, much more often with friends, children or grandchildren.

All of us recognise the desire to have fun with each other, to laugh and to party. The archetype coupled to this desire is called the Jester. At Ben & Jerry's to this day, they have cleverly tapped into this desire for their ideas. New ideas for flavours are given playful names, the packaging is fun and the commercials always contain a joke.

If you connect your idea to the Jester archetype, you in fact transmit the following message to the Black Box. **Come on, let's have some fun and celebrate life**. A message filled with positive emotions. However, as is the case with each archetype, the funny side of the Jester also has a downside to it. If you couple your idea to the Jester you run the risk of being seen as shallow. Frivolity isn't always fitting. You can't always laugh everything off and party.

ARCHETYPE
LOVER

Alfa Romeo's story shows us what funny turns startup ideas can take. Nicola Romeo, a manufacturer of pumps and compressors, purchased the failing car brand ALFA from the bank, during the First World War. Ironically, he showed no love for cars. He did, however, need production space for the manufacturing of railway materials, trucks and tractors, products he could easily sell during the war. A logic acquisition.

It wasn't until later that he came up with the idea to switch to manufacturing cars again. While the business went through deep financial recessions during the 1920s, people at the factory started thinking of the value that the concept car could represent. Maybe that was much more than simply getting from A to B.

Someone at Alfa Romeo must have come to the conclusion that car driving's success also related to a passion for speed and screeching tires. This insight led to a crucial strategic decision. The brand committed itself fully to taking part in racing events. Through great successes on the circuits, Alfa Romeo became the darling of racing fanatics in Italy and far beyond. Almost a century later, its fans still show to Alfa Romeo that driving a car is more than just a passion for speed. It can

7

also be about eye-catching design and a great engine sound. Alfa Romeo offers you a car to fall in love with, even though in the early days they would rust away from under your arse in bad weather. The brand makes clever use of people's desire to love blindly, enjoy unconditionally and adore irrationally.

If you couple your idea to the archetype Lover you are in fact saying the following. **You and me, we are both special, and we've built up an intimate relationship that is based on a mutual passion for a particular topic.** You appeal to the need to love and to enjoy yourself and the feelings associated with these needs.

The Lover, of course, has a downside too. Love is a dream that can easily be shattered if the ideal picture is damaged. In that respect, those rusty models weren't such a good idea. Alfa Romeo has been lucky that its design was so successful aesthetically and that their fans were so enormously passionate. Otherwise, the company would undoubtedly have collapsed.

ARCHETYPE
CAREGIVER

At the beginning of the 20th century, Oscar Troplowitz was a pharmacist who had some interesting ideas. In 1911 he had just launched the now world-famous lip balm Labello, when he was introduced to Isaac Lifschütz. This chemist developed an interesting emulsifier that, for the first time ever, made it possible to make a stable mix of water and oil that is easy to spread out.

It immediately gave Troplowitz new ideas. Using the emulsifier, he developed a snow white skin cream together with dermatologist Paul Gerson Unna. He used the Latin word for snow, nix or nivis, as an inspiration for the name. He used the derivative Nivea and a new brand was born. The product was an instant hit. Shops are still continuously stocked with the typical Nivea-blue containers. We will return to the significance of a recognizable colour later on in our book.

Nivea's popularity isn't exclusively due to the fact that they are great creams, deodorants, shampoos and lotions. Somewhere along the ride, an individual or a team had a revelation about the emotional value of all these blue care ideas. This must have led to the insight that another element lies behind our desire to prevent wrinkles, dandruff and smelly armpits. You may think it's

7

to remain attractive to others. Well, at Nivea they saw something different. You don't rub your baby's skin with lotion to make them sexier. You do it because you feel a strong need to care for and protect your child. A wife chooses Nivea for men if her husband is her baby. If the husband is a modern man, he can of course buy it himself. Everyone feels some kind of need to take care of themselves. Or to be cared for properly. Ask the massage industry or nursing schools; they depend on such needs.

Nivea has chosen the archetype Caregiver for their ideas. It sends the following message into the Black Box. **Don't worry, our ideas and products will care for you and protect you. We care for you or help you to care for others.** Great, right?

Well, caution is needed for Caregivers. It's a rather idealistic archetype that tends to put themselves second. Sometimes this is reflected in the fact that the investment in the idea and what you get back in return aren't in balance. In business terms: the business model sucks. A pitfall that Beiersdorf, Nivea's mother company, hasn't succumbed to. The turnover in 2019 was more than 7,6 billion USD, the profit amounted to 14,5%. This has come from brands such as Labello (still today!) and Hansaplast. It's no coincidence that these are seen as Caregivers. And Nivea is labelled the key driver of sales growth. Nivea is a pretty strong, or in any case, lucrative brand.

ARCHETYPE
EVERYMAN

Entrepreneurial types such as Ingvar Kamprad are full of ideas. As a naughty five-year-old it seemed a lucrative idea to him to sell matches. Some time later he switched to office supplies followed by furniture. He decided that catalogue sales could work well and he was right. But things really got out of hand when he figured out that it would be handy if you could buy your furniture at a place where they put it in a box that fits in your car, and which you can assemble at home.

We are, of course, talking about IKEA, which has become a huge multinational thanks to this formula.

Assembling an IKEA bookcase can be a hellish task. Our ex-colleague Berend Jan Verheijen always buys two IKEA bookcases. One to assemble and one to kick to pieces when he fails. IKEA's formula, which requires customers to do a tricky part of the work, would never have been successful, had they not thought out the value of their furniture.

IKEA's target audience is people who are down to earth and just want the same as everyone else. They are looking for an affordable, solid

7

solution without all the frills. There's a lot you can say about a Billy bookcase, but you can't say it's expensive, falls apart or stands out. But it is practical and functional.

Again and again, IKEA taps into our deep desire to conform. People aren't just social beings, but also loyal a lot of the time. They look for allies to solve challenges on the basis of equality. Quality and no nonsense are important factors.

The archetype behind this is the Everyman. This archetype is usually compared to the helpful, down to earth neighbour. We think it's a good comparison. We can just envision it. Your neighbour sees you looking at your overflowing gutter and hands you a sturdy ladder. "Come on, we'll fix this", he says. You climb up the ladder, while he holds it for you and gives you small tips along the way, without being irritating or preachy. We all want a neighbour like that.

The Everyman's message is as follows: **if you choose me, you choose a down to earth, loyal ally. We are equal and on the basis of mutual trust we aim for quality.**

Being down to earth can however be pretty boring. If there are competing ideas with the same quality that look better, you could end up losing the competition.

ARCHETYPE
INNOCENT

Smog, nitrogen, pollution... We may be ruining our planet with them, but more than a century ago the car was a rather good idea. It doesn't get tired as quickly as a horse does. It massively increased our mobility. More and more people bought a car. In many countries, the need soon arose to establish associations for all those car owners. The AAA in the United States, the AA in Great Britain and the ADAC in Germany, for example. In the Netherlands we have an association for car drivers too: the ANWB.

Pretty much everyone with a driving licence is a member of the ANWB in the Netherlands. Its success is mainly due to an attractive idea. If you're a member of the ANWB, they guarantee they'll come and assist you if your car breaks down. Not just in the Netherlands, but in the whole of Europe, depending on your contract. Including overnight stays in hotels in areas where you had no intention of staying, or replacement transportation if you've really blown up your engine.

The success of this ANWB (also called the Wegenwacht, which roughly translates as 'roadside assistance') service is based on a good value analysis of driving and travelling. The Dutch seem

7

to love nothing more than 'fleeing' their country. Not surprising, seeing as it's a nice, well organized, but also small, crowded and rainy country. You bump into Dutch people all over Europe, especially during the summer. From the North Cape to Gibraltar, you hear our language all around you. And the Dutch love to take their own car, with their own caravan attached to it.

A car offers more than just simple mobility, is what they thought at the ANWB. It's a way of travelling with your caravan to heavenly places in the South of France and Italy, Austria and Norway. The tourist is generally optimistic about the carefree weeks of holiday lying ahead of him, but is of course a bit vulnerable too. What if the engine overheats on the first mountain? You don't have mountains in the Netherlands, so how could you know that your car doesn't stand a chance with that very heavy caravan attached to the tow bar? Dutch people usually speak bad French and the French don't speak Dutch. But don't worry, of course, it won't go wrong. And if it does, you can just call the ANWB.

The ANWB taps into this sense of fear of the dream shattering to pieces by coming to the rescue. By doing this, they fully respond to the archetype Innocent. The message associated with this archetype is the following: **of course, you should enter that carefree, idyllic world with all its positive emotions. It's enriching. It makes sense**

that you are optimistic but are also aware of the risks. Situations can arise, which you can't really resolve yourself. Then it's good to know that someone has got your back. Well, if it does go wrong, we are always there to help you out.

The downside of the Innocent is that you end up patronizing the people you want to target too much. Before you know it, your idea treats adults as little children. Sometimes we don't want to know that we're helpless, it doesn't look so cool.

ARCHETYPE
RULER

It's pretty handy to be able to check what time it is every moment of the day. A wristwatch is a pretty good idea in that case. At the start of the 20th century, Hans Wildorf wasn't satisfied with the accuracy of the watches on the market. He started to have watches made that were equipped with very precise Swiss inner workings. Soon Wildorf's Rolex was the most reliable wristwatch on the market.

It can be really nice to have the time under control. It's the opposite of chaos. Wildorf looked beyond the practical side. He decided that accuracy shouldn't be at the expense of elegance. A watch could also be a piece of jewellery. He made his watches into a jewel that gave people the feeling that you were a leader with style. Dominant, in control and with a vision.

Wildorf very cleverly expanded on this insight. With each new innovation he made sure that his watches remained the point of reference. He also made his watches available to people who dominated the world through remarkable achievements. The pilot who was the first to fly over the Mount Everest got a Rolex watch. Sir Edmund Hillary, who was the first person to climb that mountain, got one too. Perfect symbolism.

These people literally dominated the world. This way Rolex raised the status of its watches to epic heights. The simple idea of wearing a watch on your wrist was transformed into a status symbol for everyone who wanted to show that they were really successful. To prove that it was a watch for powerful people, Rolex didn't even hesitate to brand one of their watch straps 'The President'.

Deep down we would all like to own a Rolex. At the very least, we would at times like to have so much confidence and influence that people would look up to us. The promise of an idea based on the archetype Ruler is: **we will help you to become and remain a leader. We will give you status, place you on a pedestal. Together we will show the world that you're someone with influence, for whom only the best is good enough.**

Are you puking yet? Arrogance is of course a pitfall with the Ruler. You can't make yourself bigger without making others seem smaller. And that is not often considered pleasant. Rulers can be big shots and assholes. Ideas that are coupled to the Ruler should take into account that certain people will loathe their idea. This doesn't have to be a problem, as long as enough people support the idea.

ARCHETYPE
SAGE

Telling stories is as old as civilization itself. People are wired for storytelling. We need it to be able to function. It's through stories that we effectively learn to understand how the world works. The stories can be fictive, exaggerated, or real. In the latter case you can even speak of the spreading of news.

A long time ago, the news was transmitted by travelling folks, based on stories. The roman emperor Julius Caesar was one of the first people to engage in the daily spreading of news. His Acta Diurna contained new daily messages that were displayed at public places in ancient Rome. State media, so to speak.

In China, newsletters were written as far back as the early Middle Ages. Quite a challenge if you wanted a wide circulation. The brilliant concept of the printing press at the end of the Middle Ages made a new idea possible: quick printing of news on paper. And so the newspaper was born. The papers Relation from Strasbourg and Avisio from Wolfsbüttel have the honour of being the oldest newspapers in the world. The birth year of the idea: 1609. After that things took off and the newspaper grew into a trusted way of making sense of what was happening in the world. The mission statement of one of the most famous newspapers in the world, The New York Times, sums up perfectly what the newspaper is all about: "We seek the truth and help people understand the world."

Many newspapers are struggling in the internet era. This is due to the fact that the printing press has been overtaken by 5G and WiFi. Not because we're less curious or eager to learn. The newspaper and many of its successors are eager to use the Sage archetype. You can envision the archetype as a teacher who enjoys investigating how the world works with his students. Each answer generates a new question. The students, in turn, are just as happy. They can revel in their curiosity. No miracle a lot of universities are based on this archetype.

An idea coupled to the Sage tells the outside world the following. **There is so much to question, to puzzle out, to research and to learn. Come on, we will follow our curiosity and together we will figure out how the world works.**

For the Sage the questions are usually more intriguing than the answer.

The Sage goes well with science. But what happens in science? It's by definition an unfinished business. There's always a new issue. Because in search of the truth the idea needs to (mostly) stay objective, it can seem rather distant, even cold.

7

Moreover, before you know it the idea is preaching on the sideline without providing a relevant contribution to essential matters. It could get on your nerves.

ARCHETYPE
MAGICIAN

The Sage provides you with an insight into how something works, but sometimes we don't actually want that. We'd rather be charmed. If you want to measure how strong that desire can be, you ought to propose to your nieces and nephews to go to Disneyland. No kids around? Go yourself. It's a magical experience for grown-ups too.

Disneyland was conceived by Walt Disney. At the end of the 1930s, as a young father, he could often be found at the merry-go-round with his daughters. This was where he first envisioned the possibility of an amusement park. But unfortunately, he was busy making cartoons and soon after, the Second World War broke out. The plan gathered dust somewhere at the bottom of a drawer and wasn't retrieved until the late 1950s. During this time Disney received quite a few letters from people wanting to visit the Disney studios. Evidently, there was a market for the idea.

Apparently, Disney was aware of the fact that his cartoons and films offered more than just simple amusement. He in fact created dreamworlds with them. He took this insight to the drawing board of Disneyland. Disney produced an amusement park that formed a fairytale-like world. People were in awe.

7

A visit is an experience that you don't need to know all the ins and outs about. You don't want to figure out the mechanics behind your experience, you just want to experience the magic.

Up until this day, Disney uses the archetype Magician for most of its ideas. These ideas often create fairytale-like surroundings that make us forget the world around us. The message: **come, let go of reality and enter our magical world. Let yourself be charmed by this remarkable experience. Don't ask questions. Just enjoy the ride.**

It's not just at Disney that they have lots of this type of ideas, the same applies to the circus, illusionists and theatre shows. A downside is that it can feel fake, a bubble that can be burst. Too good to be true. It can be nice to be fooled, but if it changes into a sense of being manipulated then you have a problem. Think about the Mickey Mouse mascot that embraces you in Main Street without your permission and you suddenly realise that inside the suit is a guy who is 1m85, who ate shawarma with garlic sauce last night. Definitely not a mouse.

ARCHETYPE
HERO

You use up energy in order to achieve a goal. If it's a physical achievement, your own engine gets to work hard. That produces heat. You sweat so that your temperature doesn't rise too much. The evaporation of the sweat on your skin gives you the coolness that you need to keep going. This works well until you run out of liquids. Soon it's done with the fun. And this happens before you know it. Try running a marathon without drinking anything. You'll probably get the point at 15 km. Especially in warm weather.

So, you need to drink. But drinking during exercising is not that easy. Before you know it, you feel sick as a dog. And don't you lose much more than just water when you're exercising vigorously? Salt to start with, but other minerals too. And what if you add a bit of sugar, for an energy boost? How much should you add?

For the average sportsman these probably aren't the most relevant questions. But they're crucial for professional athletes. That was why Roy Graves, the Florida Gators coach in 1965, posed these questions to the University of Florida College of Medicine. Was it possible to develop a drink that fully compensated that loss of fluid in his football players? The scientists got down to work and came

7

up with Gator-Aid. A drink that didn't just contain water and sugar, but also sodium, potassium and phosphate. The Gators ended up winning their first Orange Bowl on it, but the question remained whether the drink had really helped. Who knows, maybe it was just a placebo. To prevent claims, the name Aid was replaced by Ade: Gatorade.

Gatorade's sport drink was successfully marketed by appealing to people's need to bring out the best in themselves. We all set ourselves goals and experience pride and other positive emotions if we achieve them. It shows that we have perseverance and courage. Real life heroes.

Ideas based on this premise are coupled to the archetype Hero. The Hero's message is: **here you have a tool that will allow you to improve your personal best. We will help you to persevere, to improve and be courageous. This way, you will deliver the best possible performances and you will be very pleased with yourself.** Good for your self-esteem.

You should be careful though with people that want to excel. Their ego can get in the way. Especially if the performance is measurable and a tangible award awaits them at the finishing line. Tunnel vision and foul play could be just around the corner. The Hero idea can promote unethical behaviour.

ARCHETYPE
CREATOR

The camera was a fascinating idea. Suddenly you could seize the moment and capture it on paper. Shame that it was such a hell developing film. Darkroom, chemical baths, difficult to do in your attic room. So digital photography was an even better idea. Not only could you use your memory card multiple times, unlike with film, but developing was also no longer needed. You saw the result instantly and just transferred the files to your computer.

An image is created on your monitor with pixels. Smart people like Thomas Knoll realized that these pixels could easily be manipulated. Knoll got down to business with his brother and developed the first version of Photoshop in 1990. New versions appeared as the years passed, which gave photographers and designers more and more possibilities.

These days anyone that's skilled in Photoshop can transform an average shot into a masterpiece. In addition Adobe has created a whole software family that invites you to create everything you can imagine. You can make whole magazines with inDesign, logos and other vector drawings with Illustrator and do video montage with Premiere Pro.

7

If you've got something visual in mind, you can probably create it with Adobe Creative Cloud. Adobe uses Photoshop and all their other software to encourage you to make beautiful visuals. Visual self-expression has never been so accessible.

Adobe Photoshop taps into the Creator archetype. This type of ideas tells you: **we're going to help you to transform your fantasy and imagination into tangible results. Everything you can think of is possible**. This way the Creator unleashes the artist in you. Being able to express yourself and making beautiful things... People have an appetite for that.

This archetype is primarily suitable for ideas that help you to create something yourself. The risk is of course that it's all a little bit less accessible than you imagine as creator of the idea. At the end of the day, Photoshop is a complicated software package. And understanding Premiere Pro is a real headache for starting image editors. If users don't succeed, they get frustrated. Be careful what you promise as Creator, because disappointment can be just around the corner.

ARCHETYPE
EXPLORER

We've seen before how the Alfa Romeo launched their car into the Black Box successfully by framing the car as a lovable machine. It's also possible to do this in at least 11 other ways. There are a lot more car brands and archetypes. Precisely because cars are such an extension of your ego, car brands love to use archetypes to storm your Black Box. Mercedes is a ruler, Volvo a Caregiver, Toyota an Everyman, Audi a Sage and BMW a Hero. A perfect example to explain a different approach from Alfa Romeo's is the Land Rover.

In essence, a Land Rover doesn't operate much differently than an Alfa Romeo. The idea is much the same: engine, 4 wheels, steering wheel. Fine for driving from A to B. If you look harder, you can easily find differences. The tires are a lot bigger and have a much rougher profile. Of course, it looks graceless and it's got four-wheel drive. If there are forest tracks between A and B, you're much better off with a Land Rover than with an Alfa. The latter is much better for racing on tarmac, smooth as glass. So the idea has just been developed differently.

7

This is due to the fact that the Rover manufacturer came up with a very different analysis of the emotional value of the idea of the car when the Land Rover was launched in 1948. According to Rover, the car was much more than a mode of transportation from A to B. It was a tool you could use to explore the world. You could make an office clerk feel like a world explorer. On to the horizon and far beyond! Good work, because now you immediately feel like a modern-day Columbus when you step into the car.

The need to expand your horizon and go down unbeaten paths is embedded deeply in human beings. Brands that anticipate that, make use of the archetype Explorer. Like the Sage, the Explorer appeals to people's curiosity, but in a different way. Less analytical, more focused on exploring. **Come**, such a brand says, **We're going on an adventure. Let's see what there is to discover beyond the horizon.**

A very enriching attitude that gives you a sense of freedom. But it can also come across as restlessness, seeing as an explorer is never ready to hang up their boots. And anyway, which direction are you going to head in if all directions are interesting?

ARCHETYPE
OUTLAW

Forty years ago, watching TV was even more boring than it is today. There were only a few channels available, and these were filled with content that was quite interesting for adults, but rarely for teenagers. They listened to the radio instead. That changed when in 1981 Warner Amex had the following idea: what if you brought radio to the TV?

With the launch of MTV a radical new way of making TV was introduced. No longer news, game shows and sports from afternoon to evening, but non-stop music videos, 24 hours a day. Cool veejays made the picture complete. MTV was an idea that the time was ripe for. The world constantly longed for new songs from stars such as Michael Jackson, Madonna and Prince. The video editing technology had advanced just enough to produce spectacular video clips. And you could find a TV in almost all western households. Bingo!

But MTV's success was down to much more than that. According to the channel, music wasn't just a nice mix of images and sound to entertain the target audience. They also saw it as a tool for youngsters to rebel against the world around them. This approach got on like a house on fire.

7

Makes sense of course, as the target group was formed by teenagers. They are busy finding out their own identity and they do this by making the lives of others difficult. Oh, oh, oh, how differently we all behave between our fourteenth and our... Yes, when does it actually stop? Being rebellious never tires!

Outlaw ideas such as MTV unleash the rebel inside us. They use the defiance we all have in us. Now and again we would all love to shout f*ck you, or give the finger to the mainstream. Great! **Come on**, these ideas tell you. **Screw them all. We're going to do it radically differently!**

We ourselves find this type of ideas very tempting. We try not to get caught in the trap that comes with them. A revolutionary attitude can feel great, but drama and chaos are lurking. Revolutions can come at a high price. Before you know it you're fighting with every Tom, Dick and Harry. That's an essential part of it, but you need to be able to deal with it.

And now you have to make a choice. You need to apply focus in the web of emotions surrounding your newborn brand. In our eyes the choice of a single archetype is the ideal aid. You can choose from twelve archetypes, and you've got to pick one. In our experience, singling out an archetype is not as easy as you may think.

Often, multiple archetypes seem attractive. And, as we've seen before, choosing is something people find hard to do. It is, however, really important that you pick one and that you stick with your choice. To the people you need for growing your newborn brand this is nice and clear. They want to know the value of your brand. Today, tomorrow, and in a year's time.

We think that it works here just like with human relationships. You have friends that you hit the town with every weekend and have a lot of fun with (Jester). You have a mother who takes care of you (Caregiver) and a coach who helps you to get fit, with a gruelling training plan (Hero). It gets complicated if your mum suddenly wants to go to the pub with you. Or if your trainer prepares a hot water bottle for you if you're in bed with a fever. And if the friends you hang out with come and visit you, with a beer in their hand, encouraging you to do ten extra push-ups. Therefore, to prevent confusion, brands work with a clear and consistent role. They try to play that role day in and day out.

7

Maybe this question will help you make a choice. Imagine that your newborn brand is a friend. What type of friend should it be? Which promise can you use to win over your target group? What are you going to do together? Go on an adventure (Explorer), have fun (Jester) or enter a fairytale world (Magician)? The choices aren't endless: you can only pick one out of 12.

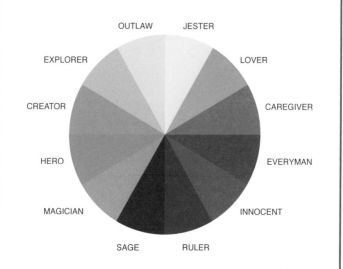

MY ARCHETYPE WILL BE:

Pick the archetype for your startup idea!

OUTLAW JESTER
EXPLORER LOVER
CREATOR CAREGIVER
HERO EVERYMAN
MAGICIAN INNOCENT
SAGE RULER

The archetype of my brand will be ...

CHOOSE YOUR
CORE VALUES

Did we just say the choice isn't endless? We'd like to come back to that. The fact that there are just twelve archetypes sometimes leads to looks of surprise. Can the world be reduced to something so simple? Can that be right? And if it's correct, how can brands and ideas still distinguish themselves from one another?

Our answer to these questions is as follows. The twelve archetypes are main categories for us. Within these categories you have endless possibilities. One Jester isn't the other. Here too we can make a striking comparison with human relations. Imagine that you and five friends often paint the town red. Dancing, partying, fun! You're all Jesters, but you're all different at the same time. One of you is melancholic, the other sarcastic and a third exuberant, and there is even one that gets rude and aggressive when drunk.

Your character determines how you give shape to the Jester. Just as every human being is unique, every brand can be unique too in their interpretation of the archetype. When you pick an archetype, you know roughly which role the brand will play for users of that brand, but you don't know yet how to give it shape. So there's a follow-up question to the question which archetype you choose for your idea: exactly what kind of Jester/Outlaw/Hero/Ruler/Caregiver/Creator/Explorer/Innocent/Sage/Magician/Everyman/Lover?

Of course, we'd love to help you embark on the next step. We suggest you supplement the archetype you've picked with three core values.

Core values can help you with your interpretation of the archetype. They help you create the unique character of your brand. They are very handy to use at a later stage in order to take the right decisions in the further development of your startup. They are also an ideal guideline for determining your topics and the tone of voice of your communications. But they provide you with much more than that. Trust.

People need to choose your brand and trust plays an important role when we make choices. In order to create trust with your brand, you can fulfill the requirements for a quality mark, rely on reviews or offer guarantees.

Another way is to determine a couple of core values for your brand and consistently live by them. As a result, your behaviour becomes predictable. Being predictable sounds boring. But that is exactly what customers of your brand find appealing. Knowing where you stand works well with people. In this case the following applies: the more consistent the better.

A brand that shouts from the rooftops that honesty is their core value won't cheat you. A brand that has politeness as its core value will always treat you decently and in a civilized manner. A brand that has innovative as its core value will keep offering you the newest solutions. A brand which is based on tolerance will never exclude you. A brand that has humour as one of its core values will always put a smile on your face.

It's important that you think hard about the core values that you want to associate with your brand. You're stuck with them for the rest of your brand's lifespan if you want to stay credible and trustworthy. You can't come up with new core values tomorrow if you're not satisfied with them after all. Everyone will become confused.

Your core values need to be appealing for the people you want to convince. They ought to be personal characteristics too. You should be able to stick the values you choose for your brand onto people. So quality is not a core value. You wouldn't say of your neighbour or uncle that they are quality. Core values are positive human characteristics such as honesty, openness, transparency and curiosity.

8

We have made a list of 128 possible core values for you. Pick three characteristics that suit your newborn brand. These will be the values that you link to your archetype. This way your brand will get a defined character: predictable, recognizable, but also authentic and unique.

Attractive, Assertive, Authentic, Autonomous, Adventurous, Thoughtful, Affordable, Gracious, Competent, Polite, Trustworthy, Modest, Decisive, Magical, Involved, Inspiring, Competitive, Consistent, Creative, Resolute, Decent, Competent, Servile, Direct, Goal-oriented, Concise, Sustainable, Simple, Honest, Effective, Efficient, Energetic, Enthusiastic, Balanced, Exclusive, Subtle, Flexible, Thorough, Daring, Equal, Believable, Nuanced, Sensitive, Healthy, Gracious, Harmonious, Passionate, Clear, Courteous, Helpful, Humorous, Empathetic, Innovative, Inspiring, Sincere, Intimate, Inventive, Youthful, Customer-oriented, Customer friendly, Studious, Personal, High-spirited, Loyal, Mild, Brave, Outspoken, Humble, Curious, Down to earth, Selfless, Self-sufficient, Flawless, Entrepreneurial, Relaxed, Unconditional, Open, Excited, Perceptive, Optimistic, Orderly, Original, Fervent, Prestigious, Professional, Rational, Fair minded, Results-oriented, Calm, Sharp, Simple, Supportive, Powerful, Playful, Spiritual, Spontaneous, Stable, Combative, Sympathetic, Tender, Content, Accessible, Dedicated, Tolerant, Traditional, Faithful, Challenging, Excellent,

*Determined, Versatile, Resilient, Safe, Responsible,
Connecting, Connected, Lenient, Groundbreaking,
Resourceful, Full of life, Careful, Happy, Dignified,
Wise, Independent, Meaningful, Meticulous,
Caring, Economical.*

Take the time to go over this long list. Consider each value briefly. Assess if you think it fits your brand. As we've said before, you should end up with three core values. That doesn't mean 2, 4 or 7. From our experience, 3 works best. With less you will be cutting corners and with more you will lose focus.

It's important to realise that the core values don't necessarily need to reflect your personal values. You can be very modest yourself and develop a brand that you want to portray as the ringleader. Kids look like their parents, but aren't their spitting image.

Can we wish you luck? Up until now you've had to make a lot of choices. This is once again a tough one. And there will be more in the next couple of steps. Choosing is losing. It hurts. But it's a must and if you choose well it puts a smile on your face.

Let's go!

8

MY THREE CORE VALUES WILL BE:

Write down the core values for your startup idea!

1. ...

2. ...

3. ...

DEVELOP YOUR
CORE VALUES

The next step is developing your core values. On paper they look like nice words, but you haven't learned much if you don't explain the significance they have for your newborn brand. You don't need to write a whole book for such an explanation. 3-5 sentences, in which you briefly explain what the core value signifies for your brand will do. We've added examples below for the core values Personal, Trustworthy and Innovative.

If it so happens that you've chosen these core values, don't copy and paste. The focus will undoubtedly be different for your own brand.

Example core value Personal

We think it's important to build up personal relationships. In our eyes, having chemistry with one another is integral to a perfect final result. We think it's essential to know who you are and what you want. So we often consult our clients and customise our products. We never want our customers to have reservations about going into business with us.

9

Example core value Trustworthy

Keeping secrets from each other is out of the question for us. We value transparency and are straightforward. We're very loyal to our customers. A deal is a deal. We take good care of anyone we work with and are clear about all details concerning our product. We ensure that everything complies with all rules and regulations.

Example core value Innovative

We use our experience and creativity to design innovative products. We create unique solutions containing elements that surprise through their smartness and earn admiration with their beauty and practicality. We aim for beautiful, smart, sustainable and handy.

Go ahead and fine-tune your 3 core values!

YOUR CORE VALUES FINE-TUNED:

Write down a short explanation of each of the three
core values.

1. ...

2. ...

3. ...

9

So, core values bring clarity and help you make choices. They ensure that you stay authentic, maintain focus and that you're trustworthy. There is, however, a downside. They make you less flexible.

Imagine you've picked economical as your core value. That means you can never again ask for a shocking amount of money for your product or service. Not even if you really need the money. A core value rules out opposite behaviour. This can be hard in some instances. That's why we refer to this phenomenon as the downside of a chosen core value.

It's smart to identify the downsides of your core values before you make your final choice. From experience, we know that you sometimes take an overly idealistic approach for your core value, only to turn pale when you become aware of the downsides. Assessing the consequences of your choices usually leads to better decisions. So, go for it and get a clear picture of the downside. We will again assist you with three examples.

Imagine that you've chosen the core value Personal. What will you rule out in that case?

> *Treating your target group as if they are anonymous or not taking them seriously. Not ringing back. Being uninterested. Ignoring complaints, massive mailings, or starting a letter with 'Dear customer'.*

Have you picked the core value Trustworthy?
Then don't even think of doing this.

>Abusing the vulnerable position of your target group. Requesting unreasonable commissions for purchased products and services. Abandoning target groups and partners. Being unclear about whatever. Not doing what you promised.

And if you've singled out Innovative as your core value then refrain from the following.

>Making an average product. Not thinking of a good solution. Not being proud of your own design. Designing something that looks good but isn't very practical at the end of the day. Coming up with something practical that isn't attractive or is worn out in no time. Developing something old-fashioned.

Does the above sound pretty obvious? Maybe. But you wouldn't believe how often things go wrong.

9

THE DOWNSIDE OF YOUR VALUES:

Describe what you will never do as a brand because of your core values.

1. ...

2. ...

3. ...

ON THE
RIGHT TRACK

Have you already been complimented by us? No? Well here you go. You're doing a great job! We're proud of you. You've already completed 9 steps. Your newborn brand is really taking shape. Cool!

If everything has gone to plan, the previous steps have ensured that you have almost completed the DNA and the character of your newborn brand.

Let's put it this way: the interior part is almost done, but you've still got a lot to do on the exterior. Let's say you're halfway. Maybe you've left the toughest part behind you. Screwing up your brand is becoming increasingly difficult. So let's crack on. On to adulthood!

iz

GET INSPIRATION
FOR THE EXTERIOR

Your brand's interior is super important for success in the Black Box. But your target group won't be able to see the interior. They will only see the exterior. So, the exterior needs to be a perfect translation of its interior. And it's a bit of a challenge to achieve this.

The next steps are aimed at creating a mix of elements which together make for an attractive, recognizable exterior that corresponds to the interior. We shall see that this concerns matters such as choosing a name, colour and symbol and developing a slogan and a unique story. Yes, we're talking about communication tools.

What exactly would we like to achieve with these communication tools? Well, here's the thing. We looked at the complex web of emotions surrounding your brand when we determined the DNA and the character of your brand. With the aid of the archetype, we applied focus. All of this was aimed at the interior.

Now the desired emotions and feelings need to be brought to the exterior, in order to transmit them to the target audience through communication tools. If this succeeds, the target group will get the required emotional click in the Black Box with your newborn brand.

Developing communication tools is a fascinating and challenging creative process. We can't wait to get to down to business. But with creativity the following always applies: you need insight and inspiration to arrive at something really good. Before we get to work, we will search for precisely that.

We now have a set of three questions for you to help you make the translation from the interior to the exterior. They may be unusual questions in your view, but believe us, they really work. Here they are:

- What type of music is your brand?

- What type of person is your brand?

- What sensory experience is your brand?

If you're able to clearly answer all these questions, you'll see that it will become much easier to make choices about the design of your communication tools. On the next few pages we will expand on these questions. And we will of course go looking for answers together.

Up until now we've mainly talked about feelings. In a way, we've treated it in a somewhat distant manner. This is the time to experience ourselves which feeling is exactly meant. We really want to feel it ourselves. This makes the design process a lot simpler and better.

Let's try and summon the right feelings and moods. There's nothing better to do this with than with music. Go figure. Blues gives you the blues. A film becomes completely devoid of emotions and therefore boring without a soundtrack. A lot of athletes boost their morale before the game with a good beat. Others seek peace with headphones and classical music and relax on a yoga mat.

Research has shown that music is a universal language. It can very specifically evoke emotions and feelings. You have no idea what lights up on a brain scan if you put on music. Because music works so well at evoking feelings, people have used music for as long as we remember to create a good atmosphere. Music is essential at a party, but also at a funeral or an election event. Every feeling has accompanying music. So...**What type of music is your idea?**

Ask yourself which music your idea can be compared to. You can think in genres, such as garage rock, happy hardcore, rap or R&B. Our feeling with this book, for example, has been upbeat poprock. Strong, but accessible and easy to dance to. Challenging, but containing a message and a touch of humour. Hopefully you'll share that feeling with us.

You can also go a step further and link it with a composer, band or artist. Bach gives you a different feeling than Bob Dylan or Lady Gaga. Or you can even define a specific symphony or hit that perfectly summarises your idea. For this book, we've had endless discussions to establish if it's All for nothing by Kensington or the chorus to Breakfast at Tiffany's. We stopped when we started squabbling.

We can of course try and figure out which beat equals which feeling. It's all been looked into and established by now. But we think it's unnecessary. This question is about your idea and your intuition. You don't need an explanation. Happy Spotifying!

10

THE MUSIC OF MY STARTUP IS:

Style: ...

Artist / Band / Composer: ...

Album / Concert: ...

Song: ...

Spotify / YouTube link: ...

The second question we want to present you with is as follows. Right from the first pages of this book we have explained to you that the relationships between brands and people resemble the relationships between people. So why would we not view the brand itself as a human being? Let's just personify it for 100 percent. The question to ask yourself is this: **what type of human is my newborn brand going to be**?

This is a whole different question from the question we have tackled before: what is my target group? Don't mix things up otherwise you will become confused.

You can just try to describe your human brand. An important first step is the sex of your brand. Is it a man or a woman? Put aside your political correctness for the moment. You're allowed to use male and female stereotypes here. Please do. We're looking for associations and feelings that people should have with regard to your brand, and we're not going to discuss whether women are gentler than men.

A second important choice is age. A brand can portray the balance and wisdom of a smart 60-year-old. Or the eagerness of a career driven 30-year-old who hasn't yet been disappointed by life. Or the freshness and bounciness of a clueless teenager. The same thing applies again: yes, this is stereotyping and that's OK. Maybe it's a must.

10

What follows is obvious. You can shape the person however you want. Hobbies, clothing, level of education, lifestyle, appearance. Come up with something that really suits your newborn brand. Again, we've answered this question for our book. We hope that this book is all the things that we aren't. A slightly better version, so to speak. Man, early forties, good-looking, well dressed, sympathetic, loved, valued for his sense of humour...

Another very good way is to look for pictures. It really is a cliché, and maybe that's because it's true. A picture says more than a thousand words. Grab your computer and log into a website with stock images. Search until you have found the person that truly embodies the feeling of your brand.

THE TYPE OF PERSON

Describe the type of person that gives you the same feeling as your newborn brand should give to your target audience. Think of age, sex, level of education, lifestyle, appearance, photo, etcetera.

...

Feelings and emotions don't just come from nowhere. They are a result of sensory perception. You see or hear something, and suddenly you start laughing or crying. If you go to a party blindfolded and wearing noise-cancelling headphones, you'll probably miss out on all the fun. Our senses and feelings are inextricably linked to each other. That's why it's interesting to find the sensory experiences that evoke the feeling you're after. We've already tackled two of our senses, sight and hearing, in the previous two questions. The music question was about listening. The personification question was mostly about seeing. That means there are three senses left.

How does your brand smell?

Smell is, so they say, a highway to emotions. Smells are usually very associative. Years later, you still know which smell was associated with a particular situation and how it made you feel. So, does your brand smell like fresh blossom, an aged port, fresh coffee, homemade apple pie, a freshly mowed lawn, the woods after a summer shower or a mix of pinewood and eucalyptus in the sauna? Or something else?

What does your brand taste of?

Taste is strongly related to smell and also easily summons up emotions. Does your brand taste like coffee made from freshly ground beans, refreshing chewing gum, peppermint, a sickly sweet energy drink, a tender steak of Wagyu beef, a Barolo that has been aging for the last ten years, or something else?

How does your brand feel when you touch it?

Emotions also arise through touch. Is your brand cold metal, wood that has been sanded, super soft velvet, springy dawn, a nice hot water bottle, a luxurious armchair that you can flop into, seat heating in your car? Or something else?

You'll see that you can often combine things when answering these questions. A brand can feel, smell and look like a fresh, warm, green lawn which has just been mowed, under a cloudless sky with a low hanging autumn sun, where a soft breeze plays with a couple of dancing, orange oak leaves. Or like diving into a very blue, ice-cold lake with sheets of ice floating around. Or like drinking a cappuccino on a nice summer morning on the terrace of a bakery, at a gently awaking Italian village square.

Your description is heading in the right direction if a clear picture is starting to form in your head. It's no surprise then that we call this a mental image. Therefore, try and describe the situation as visually as possible.

THE SMELL, TASTE AND FEEL

My brand smells like: ...

My brand tastes like: ...

My brand feels like: ...

Done? Then we can give the things that show your brand to the outside world a face. Apart from making a connection on the level of feelings and emotions, we want to strive for something else. We're aiming for recognisability.

The ambition to make brands recognisable is probably as old as humans. We give brands names, colours and symbols. For example, the idea of a bunch of European countries to cooperate on numerous subjects has been given the name European Union (EU). A pretty interesting idea, which has definitely provided trade benefits and may have even prevented wars.

It has been given the colours blue and yellow. The symbol has been made up of twelve stars in a square, placed in such a way that they form a circle.

Very handy, the recognisability that has been created. If we come across the name EU or its logo, we don't need to think about which organization is behind it. We know this immediately. Moreover, multiple associations will immediately come to mind. What we think of the EU will immediately be activated. Our Black Box gets a tremendous boost.

And if we're not quite sure, then we can fall back on something other than names, colours and symbols. The EU also has a motto. In varietate concordia. This is Latin for unity in diversity.

10

Smart, this way it only takes one sentence to know what the EU represents.

Of course, the EU is a whopper of a brand. But really, this also works for smaller brands. Colours, names, symbols and mottos make your newborn brand recognisable, unique and attractive. Very effective in the Black Box. So let's get to work!

NAME
YOUR BRAND

The first thing you do with a baby is give it a name. Often parents already have decided on a name before the baby is born. This can feel like a logical first step with baby brands too. It wouldn't surprise us if you already have a name.

But what's in a name? Wasn't Shakespeare right with his statement in Romeo & Juliet? "That which we call a rose by any other name would smell as sweet?"

Sorry, William, we think it does actually make a difference. It's really important to have a good name for your newborn brand. Every day everyone is overloaded with a mass of information. In this mass, a brand with a name that sounds good stands out much better. A powerful name aids you in the Black Box.

The question is: when is a name powerful? This question is hard to answer. There isn't a list of hard criteria. Agencies that earn a lot of money thinking up names do have several starting points and principles. We'd like to guide you through some of these principles. They can help you come up with a good name, if you don't already have one. If you do have a name in mind, then you have a good yardstick to test its strength.

Principle 1: keep it short.

Even though the Red Hot Chili Peppers and I can't believe it's not butter won't agree, short names work better than long names. One syllable starting with the letter B, that's what we consider the most powerful. Bux and Binck, for example, are very powerful names in the European financial sector. Bud is a great name for a beer.

Principle 2: stand out.

Challenging in times like these, seeing as there are already so many names. Try to stand out with your name. A striking name sticks with people much better.

If you have a lot of competition, we advise you to be original and go look for a name that is somewhat more unusual in your playing field. In the early days of the mobile phone, the market in our country was filled with names that had a connection with the product they were offering or were an old abbreviation. Vodafone, T-mobile, KPN and Telfort, for example. And then suddenly, the brand Ben popped up. No link with the product, but a completely different approach: a human name. In parts of the world it could be your neighbour's name. And short and starting with a B too.

Principle 3: easy to pronounce.

A name that is easy to pronounce has a positive effect on potential investors and customers. Apparently, without realizing it, we don't like funky things. So striking, yes, but what we don't know, we fear, so don't overdo it by stringing a bunch of crazy letters together. It may seem funny and often stands out, but it simply doesn't work well.

Principle 4: keep the option open of going international.

Consider how international you want to go. Or would like to go. A great name in your mother tongue can mean something very strange in another language. Foolish. Shocking. Laughable.

We still think the Mitsubishi Pajero is a great example. Mitsubishi introduced the Pajero four-wheel drive in the 1980s. In Spanish, however, Pajero means wanker. Unique? No. There has also been a Ford Pinto. Pinto means a little willy in Brazilian street language. And then we haven't even got started yet on the Lancia Marica. Sounds roughly like gay in Spanish. It's not great for sales to couple a car name to a sexual activity or preference. So, find out what your brand name means in other languages. Google Translate is your friend.

11

Principle 5: sustainable.

Try and look for a name that can last a long time. We frequently see the strangest names pass by, kind of like fashion trends. Nice at first, but difficult in the long run. Also, beware of names with a year in them. It can make your brand seem dated. A year isn't going to be any good until 100 years later. And only then with a product that's been made in a traditional way.

Principle 6: non descriptive.

We're not supporters of trying to describe your ideas in your brand name. There are different reasons for this. As time passes your product can change through technical innovations or whatever. Your name can then lose its right of existence. On top of that, descriptive names are hard to register as brand names.

Principle 7: don't use your own name.

Don't use your own name if you have big growth ambitions. It will make your idea come across to your target group as small and not very ambitious.

Those were the 7 principles. Just bin them now.

Principles are there to ignore. The world is full of examples of strong brand names that don't conform to these principles. John Deere is simply a personal name. Oscillococcinum is almost impossible to pronounce and still successful. 7-Eleven seems really descriptive but is hardly a small chain, with 71,000 locations in eighteen countries.

If you think you've hit the jackpot and have commercial intentions with your brand, check immediately if your name is already registered somewhere. You can find brand registers online for different geographical areas and countries. But googling the name can also give you a lot of clarity.

Some advice from us: reserve at least one week for coming up with a name. During this week you will work on it at different moments, writing down the names that come into your head. Play with them. Think of variations. Carry on until you have a long list. As the timeframe draws to a close, you do the opposite. Don't make the list longer, make it shorter. You continue this until you have only one left. This will be your name for the time being. If it survives a couple of tests with your target group and it doesn't come up against any legal problems, then it's a keeper. If not, return to the drawing board.

MY LIST OF POTENTIAL BRAND NAMES

...

...

...

...

...

...

...

...

...

...

...

...

...

...

...

...

...

...

...

...

CHOOSE YOUR
BRAND COLOURS

You've decided which values fit your brand. You've put feeling into it by deciding what type of music your brand is, what it feels like and maybe even what it smells like. And, you also have a name. Funny right, your newborn brand is really starting to become a little human being. And the development continues. We think that the colours that correspond to your brand are relevant. That's why this step focuses on the following: which colours suit your brand the best and will also do well in the Black Box?

This is not just a simple, gosh, I kind of like these colours, so I will use them. Nope. Because colour is much more than merely an aesthetic choice. You can influence others with colour. Several studies focusing on the psychology of colour have shown that colours have an important impact on people's feelings, their processing of information and their behaviour.

The right colour combination for your brand can also help you in building relationships with the people that are interesting for your brand. Colours don't just produce emotions, but also lead to recognition. There are countless companies

12

that we can recognize in a split second due to the colours they consistently use. Coca Cola red for example or Facebook blue or Easyjet orange.

Thinking about using the right colour is not something novel. Scientific insight concerning the psychology of colour already occurred at the beginning of the 19th century. During these times, scientists speculated that colour could summon up certain negative or positive emotions. The German poet, philosopher and diplomat Johan Wolfgang von Goethe spoke of plus (yellow, red-yellow, yellow-red) and minus (blue, red-blue, blue-red) colours. Plus colours would generate positive feelings such as liveliness, ambition and warm feelings. Minus colours, on the other hand, would result in negative feelings such as restlessness, fear and cold feelings.

Other psychologists thought more in terms of warm and cold colours. According to the American psychologist Jacob Naksian, we have generally come to accept the perception that warm colours, such as orange, yellow and most of all red have an arousing effect on our behaviour and lead to happiness. Blue and green, on the other hand, have a soothing effect. Psychiatrist Kurt Goldstein looked into stimulation and action as a result of warm and cold colours. Primarily through clinical observations, he experienced that the warm colours red and yellow were stimulating and produced powerful actions. The cold colours green and blue proved to be relaxing and produced calm and stable actions.

In conclusion, colours and emotions are inextricably linked. And creating emotions is just what we wanted to do. Take another look at your onliness statement and grab your archetype and your three core values. Then, let's broadly run through a couple of colours and their accompanying emotions. After that you will choose the colours that you think really go with your brand and your archetype.

Yellow: happiness and fun.

The colour of the cover of this book! Yellow is the colour of the sun, the colour of light, and mainly has positive connotations. In psychology the colour symbolizes happiness and joy of the mind, but if you're confronted with it too much, it represents anger. Yellow also corresponds to joy, optimism, prosperity and friendship and can also be associated with excitement. If you mainly want to radiate positivity and happiness, then yellow can be an interesting main colour for you. We often see Jesters choose yellow.

Red: warmth, strength and danger.

People often think that the colour red mainly invokes negative feelings in people. But red is also associated with happiness. It's an intense colour that has a vibrant and powerful influence on someone's personality and feelings. Red has got a strong association with warmth, fire or passion and with attack and conquering. Many Lovers use red. And yes, red also symbolizes negative concepts: arrogance, danger, blood, war and anger. You should mostly see red as a colour of movement so it can be interesting for you if you have a brand which you want to use to get people moving.

Green: youth, health and nature.

Green has got many positive meanings in the psychology of colour. Green represents growth, renewal, nature, youth, health, stability, creative intelligence and a balanced and youthful spirit. It's often used by Explorers and Creators. There are also associations with self-preservation. The colour green is often used as a sales tool. Take a good look around you. Green is often used to make products seem sustainable, balanced or healthy. So the colour green offers you many possibilities. But watch out, a lot of brands use green to engage in 'greenwashing'. This means that they pretend to be greener than they really are.

Blue: loyal and calm.

Blue, the colour of the ocean, the air and water. It's a cooler, non-threatening colour. It has a calming effect on the mind and symbolizes calmness, trust and wisdom, authority, generous

wealth, conservatism and trustworthiness. A
good example of the use of blue are the logos of
the police and the government in many countries.
Their blue colour represents authority and the
trustworthiness these agencies need to radiate. It
really is a colour for the Ruler and the Innocent.

Black and white: strength versus calmness.

Black is super powerful. It can be professional,
stylish and elegant. It can also have mystical or
negative connotations. Think of black magic or
black clothing which is associated with mourning
in a lot of cultures. The colour white represents
calmness. But it also symbolises youth, innocence,
truth, orderliness and humility. It also stands
for balance and neutrality. And mind you, it
represents also mourning in quite a few Asian
cultures. So, use black if you want to be seen as
strong and professional and white for a neutral and
balanced appearance. Quite a few Outlaws aim for
the contrast between black and white and use the
combination.

Are you beginning to get a feeling of the colour
that would suit your startup? OK, we will help you
just a little bit more. We have added an overview
for you, containing the most common colours, the
associations they evoke and which famous brands
use these colours. This table is our own summary
distilled from a number of more or less reliable
internet sources. Use it to your advantage.

12

Colour	Association	Examples
	Love, anger, passion, hunger	McDonalds, Coca Cola, Vodafone
	Hope, happiness, energy, optimism	Ikea, Snapchat, Nikon
	Trustworthiness, safety, reliability	Facebook, HP, Oral B, LinekdIn
	Stability, calmness, health, balance	Landrover, Starbucks
	Enthusiasm, fun, playfulness	Fanta, Easyjet, Nickelodeon
	Wisdom, luxury, power, independence	Hallmark, Milka
	Simple, sustainability	Nespresso, UPS, M&M's
	Classic, prestige, value, timeless	Adidas, Chanel
	Clean, pure, sterile	Apple
	Diversity, big, joyful	Google, Microsoft
	Wise, neutral, professional	Wikipedia, Mercedes-Benz
	Charme, romance, innocent flirting	Victoria's Secret, ICI Paris XL

Once you've chosen your colours, it's wise to check two things. We dub the first the combicheck. If you've only picked one colour, this isn't relevant, but if you have multiple colours in mind then it's a relevant question. Do these colours form a nice combination? A lot of people can determine this themselves. But not everyone. Are you one of those people that always wears the wrong jumper with the wrong trousers? Then you should ask your fashionable niece. She'll know. Another solution: check if it's a much-used combination. Autumn colours and pastels always go together nicely. That's why they're often combined that way.

You could call the second check the cultural check. Especially if you think your brand should connect with a specific target group, it's a good idea to do this check. It can prevent painful blunders, seeing as colours can have strong cultural values. Our own Fontys University shows how easily it can become uneasy. They once chose the combination yellow and purple. Your eyes probably can't take much more than that, combination-wise. The intentions were good. Purple stands for knowledge and wisdom. But purple is also the colour of mourning in the Far East and in Mexico the colour yellow apparently produces feelings of sadness. So, not a happy choice for the department of international relations. The yellow disappeared after some time, by the way, and was replaced by white. Much better.

12

You may be thinking: what are those colours for? The answer is simple: use them wherever you can. It's the basis for your brand's visual identity. Maybe after reading this book you will decide to create a Facebook or LinkedIn profile for your newborn brand. Or a website or Instagram timeline. Or send out letters the old-fashioned way. These are all instances where you should use the colours of your choice.

Be precise. One orange isn't the next. Specific colours have been given specific colour numbers. Use special software like Photoshop or a colour chart to determine which colour numbers match your colours. Be careful, there are a lot of different classifications that are used for different applications. CMYK or PMS for print for example and RGB for screen applications. With paint they often use RAL. Look up the numbers, write them down and store them somewhere safe. It will be a hell of a lot easier in the future, when someone working with you asks you what the exact colours are.

THE COLOURS OF MY BRAND

Note down the colours of your brand.

Colour 1: ...
CMYK:
RGB:
RAL:
PMS:

Colour 2: ...
CMYK:
RGB:
RAL:
PMS:

Colour 3: ...
CMYK:
RGB:
RAL:
PMS:

Colour 4: ...
CMYK:
RGB:
RAL:
PMS:

12

CHOOSE
YOUR FONTS

For a long time, people thought your handwriting said something about your personality. Companies spent a lot of money hiring analysts to draw conclusions from the handwriting of job applicants.

Later on in time, when science took another hard look, it all turned out to be bullsh*t. Messy people can write neatly and vice versa. As reader we tend to think that messy people have messy handwriting. This is an interesting point when we extend this to computer fonts. Our choice of a particular font impacts how our reader perceives our brand. A cheerful looking font will lead to a cheerful image, whereas a robust font will come across as powerful. In other words, you can make fonts do the work for you if you want to inspire the right feelings with your idea.

These days, every standard computer contains a bunch of fonts. Some fonts work very well for short slogans or headlines, others are more suitable for long pieces of text. We recommend you choose two different fonts. One for if you want to shout out a short text and one for if you want to explain something in detail.

It's worthwhile going through the fonts on your computer and rating them on the feeling they provoke. After that, select the default fonts for the written communication (stationery) which you will use for your brand. Before you get cracking with your selection, we'd like to give you some basic knowledge on fonts. They don't come in different shapes and sizes for no reason. There are in fact actual font families.

First of all, you've got the serif fonts. These fonts have small brackets. Times New Roman is a well-known example of such a font. Serif fonts are easy to read in long stories, that's why not just the Times, but also a lot of other newspapers have used them for years. They come across as classic, professional, serious, clinical, authoritative and institutional.

You also have fonts without those brackets. These are called the sans-serif fonts. They don't have strokes or brackets. These fonts generally appear modern, slick, progressive, elegant, smooth and cosmopolitan. Arial is a very well-known example as well as Helvetica. On screens, the sans-serif fonts work better than their serif friends, this is something to be mindful of.

The third family is formed by the so-called script fonts. They often look like stylish manuscripts, but they can also be very playful. Lucida is a well-known example. Script fonts produce strong emotions. The downside is that they're hardly ever suitable for a longer text. The readability can really pose a problem.

The same applies to the last family that we will discuss here: the display fonts. These are powerful, often wild and loud fonts. Very suitable for, you guessed it, use on displays. And as a header of course. But not for a long text.

Certain archetypes form a nice and logical combination with a font family. Nine out of ten times a serif font will be chosen by the Sage. An Innocent? Much more likely a sans-serif. You often see script fonts with Jesters. Because Outlaws love to shout out that they're different, you see a lot of display fonts there.

Find two fonts on your computer that you think go with the feeling you want your brand to convey. If your computer doesn't come with many fonts, or if you don't find anything appropriate, you can resort to online databases such as 1001 Freefonts, Googlefonts or Dafont. Once you've made a selection, check if they also form a nice combination visually. You can then use them together in a brochure, ad or flyer. For example, a sans-serif font for the headers and the serif font for the body text.

Check, double check. Take a look at Step 5 again. The analysis of your competitors. Handy to check again that you don't happen to have the same fonts as them. Better safe than sorry.

THE FONTS OF MY BRAND

Write down the names of the two fonts of your brand
and why you have chosen them.

Font 1: ...

Font 2: ...

13

DESIGN
YOUR SYMBOL

Name, colours, fonts. We're going to advance to the next step. Creating a symbol for your newborn brand. A symbol also creates a unique piece of the DNA of your brand. An interesting symbol ensures recognisability and allows you to stand out. And yes, symbols also work well for that magic Black Box.

The desire to couple symbols to brands must be a deep human desire because it happens all the time. We will give you a couple of recognisable examples picked from a stock of billions of ideas.

The startup idea is to sail the seas in a boat with a bunch of lads, raiding other boats and stealing their cargo, after which you all sit around drinking rum under a palm tree.

The startup idea is to provide worldwide emergency aid in disaster and conflict zones. By the way, because of its religious significance, in Islamic countries this cross is replaced by a moon.

The startup idea is to make everyone collective owners of all production facilities and to let everyone produce according to ability and consume based on needs.

The idea is to spare men and women the awkward encounter of bumping into each other on the toilet.

The idea is to warn people of the dangers of radioactivity.

The previous symbols are pretty much universally known. Imagine the power your brand's symbol can have.

Its strength doesn't just stem from its recognisability. A good symbol yields associations in a split second, which means you don't have to name them explicitly each time. As the saying goes, a picture says more than a thousand words.

Due to their power, symbols play an important role in cultures. They're the most visible embodiments of shared values, standards and the behaviour of groups of people. The interesting thing is that these people have the tendency to use cultural symbols to show what they identify with. A lot of Catholics wear a crucifix for example. Companies make clever use of this reflex. What about Apple computers and Canyon racing bikes who give you a sticker of the company image as a gift with your purchase. This really goes beyond the plastic bag you used to get at the supermarket. That had a function. You can't really do anything with a sticker. The only function for fans is that you're given the opportunity to show that you're a follower of the ideology of the brand. A fan of the brand, so to speak.

The companies mentioned apparently do the same thing as you and us. They ask themselves how they can enter into relationships with the people they need to achieve growth. They're already so far along in this that they've started tackling the question of how they can get these people to work for them. Who knows, maybe you can do that too. On the day that people proudly place a sticker of your brand on who knows what, your brand will have become more than mature. This won't be the case for the time being, but there's nothing in the way to stop you choosing a symbol for your brand.

If you're really ambitious with your brand, you will need to design a brand logo, like all brands do. You will see that this doesn't come easy. Graphic design really is a special skill, especially where logos are concerned. This is one of those elements where Pim Stuurman's three-hour law is applicable again. If you don't have the talent or skill set, ask someone else to do it for you or hire someone. Make sure the designer is up-to-date with everything you've done in the previous steps, then he or she will have all the guidance and inspiration he or she needs for a great result.

14

For those who want to try it themselves, we have nine tips.

1. First, figure out the shapes of your logo. Then, take a look at the letters (if you want to use them). The brain seems to work the same way in processing information.
2. Think about the associative power of the shapes. A round shape feels differently than an angular one.
3. The mind likes symmetry and balance. Good logos don't topple due to one side being 'heavier'.
4. Make sure that you're also able to use your logo on a dark background in the future.
5. Be mindful of the fact that you may want to print or embroider your brand onto textile later on. So don't make it too fiddly.
6. Don't forget which colours you've chosen. Using different colours now is a bit strange.
7. Think of the fact that there could be situations in which you want to be able to use your logo in gray or black and white.
8. Think about what will happen if you make your logo really large or really small.
9. Try and keep it simple. Good logos usually come from the less is more doctrine.

Ask yourself which unexpected associations people can have with your logo. Or even better: do a test round. We once discovered that a logo we had conceived for an idea that had to do with making a customer experience visible was (and we're not joking) associated with semen.

If you lack all kind of inspiration or hate abstract shapes you could think of the following. Try to discover inspiration around you. A tool for example. The hammer and sickle representing communism are just ordinary tools. Something from nature is a possibility too. In Portugal in 1974, they used carnations successfully to symbolise a revolution and in 2003 they used roses in Georgia for the same purpose. Flowers can have a impressive effect due to their associative power. But be careful that the flower you choose doesn't represent death, unless you happen to have a morbid startup idea.

The associations we have with animals are probably even more powerful. That's why animals maybe do an even better job as symbols. Wil Michels, one of our ex-colleagues and a well-known author of management literature on communication, once told us the story of a communication agency that only posed one question when designing logos for organisations. What animal does the organization resemble? Based on the answer, the logo turned out to be a lion, a gazelle, a rabbit, or whatever animal.

You can look for a symbol more closely related to you. There are quite a few political ideas that have a movement of a body part as a symbol. A fist in

14

the air for example, a hand on the heart, or both.
A particular hand gesture is also an option, the
peace sign for example. Take a look at teenagers.
It seems like they're always thinking up their own
symbolic greetings.

THE SYMBOL OF MY BRAND

Let's give it a shot! Draw your symbol (or hire someone to do it for you).

14

STEP 15

DETERMINE YOUR
TONE OF VOICE

The next step is to determine your brand's voice. It's important to find out how you think and feel the so-called tone of voice of your brand should be.

Pay attention. Nothing is right or wrong, but based on the previous steps you should now have an idea or feeling about how your brand sounds. Again, focus on your brand rather than on yourself and your own preferences. Of course there can be an overlap. Look at us. We don't just make cheesy jokes in this book, we do it in real life too.

In order to determine the tone of voice of your brand, we will give you five questions. The answers will set you in the right direction. Subsequently, we'll ask you again to go back to your chosen archetype. Why? The choice of an archetype gives you direction for your tone of voice. Each archetype speaks differently and uses different words.

Here are the five questions.

1. Does your brand speak formally or informally? Instantly a rather important difference, as how you address someone defines to some extent the relationship you've got in mind.
2. Does your brand speak professionally or relaxed? In other words, does it speak pretty business-like or rather as friends together?
3. Does your brand speak seriously or with a lot of humour? Does your brand sometimes make a joke, or does its tone always remain serious?
4. Does your brand speak reservedly or with a lot of warmth? Does it use soft language, or is it somewhat restrained?
5. Does your brand speak very maturely or youthfully? Do you hear a teenager speaking or a 40-year-old woman?

15

THE TONE OF VOICE OF MY BRAND

Answer the five questions! Does your brand speak...

1. Formally or informally?

2. Professionally or relaxed?

3. Seriously or with humour?

4. Reservedly or with warmth?

5. Maturely or youthfully?

What you need next is a vocabulary. In step 7 you picked your archetype. You've realized now that your choice gives direction to your newborn brand. In order to determine your brand's vocabulary, you can rely on your choice. Each archetype has its own vocabulary. So we've done some extra work for you. For each archetype we've compiled 50-100 words that could match the archetype's vocabulary. Get inspired. And don't hesitate, add to it yourself.

Jester

Party – Fun – Comical – Crazy – Funny – Laughing – Hip
Great – Cool – Kick – The shit – Celebration – YOLO
Live – Garlands – Gathering – Cheers – Lalala – Balloons
Great work – Whatever! – Practical Joke – Simple
Easy – Dancing – Music – Festival – Beat – DJ – Podium
Congratulations – Beach – Palm tree – Hammock
Cocktail – Champagne – Uncorking – No worries
Fireworks – Swinging – Rhythm – Singing – Clapping
Smiling – Giggling – Hilarious – Laughing out loud
Friend – Who cares? – Carpe Diem – The small hours
Hipster – Big deal! – Delicious! – You go girl! – Fiesta
Santé! – Later! – Hangover – Smiley – Thumbs up
Happy – Chuckle – Joking around – Pleasure – Bash
Roaring out with laughter – Mischief – Naughty – Rascal
Mocking – Bad – Bad boy – Cheeky

Lover

Loving – Love – Passion – Craftsmanship – Revelling
Enjoy – Like – Beautiful – Appreciate – Cool – Pure – Stylish
Design – Layout – Nice – Gorgeous – Good – Enjoyable
Beautiful – Class – Artisan – In love – Intense – Delicious
Arty – Art work – Like a painting – Masterly – Masterpiece
Authentic – Handmade – Original – Unique – Real – Wow
Heart – Pearl – Art – Designed – Focused – Jewel
With a lot of detail – Sublime – Gold – Silver – Bronze
Colourful – Scented – Feeling like – Precision
Looking forward to – Longing for – Souvenir – Fine – Quality
Lovin' it – Artisanal – Gem – Decorative – Heart – Tasteful
Magnificent – Excellent – Amazing – Sweety – Chique
Elegant – Gracious – Aesthetic – Attractive – Irresistible
Sparkly – Fine – Comfortable – Adoringly – Seductive
Tender – Alluring – Soft

Caregiver

Care – Protection – Protecting – Giving – Guarding
Babysitting – Taking off someone's hands – Solving
Caring – Carefree – Cared for – Trust – Taking over
Being sure of – Guaranteeing – Guarantee – Service
Providing – Fine – Smooth – Soft – Pamper – Assure
Protection – Cover up – Save – Defend – Encourage
Support – Reserve – Especially for you – Assist
Extending a hand – Safeguarding – Benefit – Sweet
Considerate – Saving – Accommodate – Kind – Careful
Be serviceable – Protecting – Sure – Security – Safety
Calm – Peaceful – Stability – Hope – Belief

Everyman

Normal – Down to earth – Treading carefully – Tip – Doing
Honest – Trustworthy – Friend – Neighbour – Help – Helping
It can be helpful – Solving – Simple – Easy
Accessible – Available – Basic – Basis – Everybody
Everyone – Decent – Trust – Attention – Competent
Quality – Imperturbable – Contemplative – Equal
Equipoised – Similar – Balanced – No nonsense
Grounded – Calm – Available – Approachable – Admissible
Attainable – Open – Always – Sensitive – Sensible
Suitable – Competent – Capable – Suited – Skilled
Handy – Uncomplicated

Innocent

Transparent – Solid – Optimistic – Progressive – Idealistic
Original – Positive – Efficient – Energy – Honest – Passion
Strength – Thorough – Knowhow – Support – Loyal
Personal – Perfect – Cooperating – Expertise – Trust
Sophisticated – Together – Nice – Details – Independent
Integrity – Specialist – Meaningful – Fitting – Loyal – Caring
Fun – Idealism – Friendly – Steady – Honest – Solutions
Calm – Values – Norms – Perseverance – Unique – Special
Aesthetic – Challenges – Beautiful – Appropriate – Open
Thorough – Collective – Responsible – Tailored – Accessible
Constructive – Respectful – Thoughtful – Believable
Innovative – Future-oriented – Customer-oriented – Attention
Understanding – Professional – Smart – Handy – Happy
Involved – Active – Clarifying – Comprehensive
Skillful – Sustainable

15

Ruler

Best – First – Vision – Leader – Market leader – Important
Essential – Crucial – Top – Foremost – First-rate
Ringleader – Master – Responsible – Structure – Neat
Decent – Thorough – Deep – Extensive – Meticulous
Accurate – Detailed – Punctual – Strict – Dedicated
Encompassing – Grand – Ambitious – Totally – Exact
Loyal – Pure – Fundamental – Sound – Serious
Sustainable – Indestructible – Close – Massive
Well-prepared – Punctual – Detailed – Unrelenting – Firm
Courageous – Loyal – Honourable – Intimate – Exact
Carefully – Accurate – Conscientious – Rigorous – Power
Fine – Mighty – Strong – Decent – Domination – In charge
Influence – Potential – Authority – Control – Helmsman
Captain – Rule – Ruler – Control – Master – Lieutenant
Governor – Sovereign – Superior – President – King

Sage

Question(s) – Question Mark – Study – Researching
Finding out – Summarising – Questioning – Looking
Figure out – Details – Perceptive – Philosophy – Pondering
Thinking – Thought – Theory – Science – Professional
Expert – Specialist – Source of information – Expertise
Knowledge – Knowledge centre – Knowledge hub
University – Learning – Understanding – School – Pupil
Teacher – Analysing – Unravelling – Investigating – Viewing
Looking at – Examining – Observing – Overthinking
Taxing – Contemplating – Practicing – Exploring
Checking out – Verifying – Gauging – Testing – Hypothesis

Synergy – Surveilling – Observing – Interpreting – Statement
Revising – Grounds – Unpick – Outdated – Truth
Discovering – Data – Information – Facts – Factuality
Realities – Reality – Bias – Pureness – Statistic – Validity
Representativity – Traces – Detective – Search – Taste
Examining – Examination

Magician

Magical – Fairytale – Fairytale-like – Dream – Dreams
Daydreaming – Immersing – Theatre – Film
Film-like – Clouds – Flying – Gliding – Sparkling
Enchanted – Enchanting – Dream world – Illusion
Paradise – Heavenly – Rollercoaster – Sage – Magician
Fasten your seatbelts – Doing magic – Bewitching
Magical power – Imagination – Phantasising – Musing
Fiction – Envisioning – Dream image – Fable – Story
Utopian – Myth – Surrendering – Magic – Chronic – Legend
Fairy – Experience – Flaming – Shiny – Resplendent
Gleaming – Genius – Dragon – Attractive – Energetic
Cheerful – Gnome – Happy – Eternal – Phantasy – Elf

Hero

Brave – Target – Scoring – PR – Record – Winning
Goal – Objective – Hero – Courageous – Equipment
Tools – Training – Plan – Match – Triumph – Great – Medal
Groundbreaking – Top – Achievement – Performance
Daring – Tough – Cool – Unyielding – Opponent – Gallant
Manly – Strong – Fearless – Prepared – Daring – Goodly

15

Crushed – Heroism – Heroic – Resolute – Rude – Bold
Ambition – Ambitious – Focus – Focused – Striving – Benefit
Destiny – Finish Line – Finish – Strategy – Marathon
Aspiration – Duel – Derby – Show of strength
Clash of the titans – Ruffs – Gun Smoke – War – Battlefield
Weapon – Tactic – Shooting – Holding up – Persevering
Biting the bullet – Persisting – Sprinting – Succeeding
Conquering – Triumphing – Laureate – Triumph
Winning – Harvesting

Creator

Resourceful – Sophisticated – Ingenious – Surprising
Refreshing – Driven – Inspired – Enthusiastic – Dedicated
Lively – Implementing – Achieving – Delivering – Doing
Completing – Building – Making – Forming – Creating
Designing – Thinking – Generating – Laying out – Producing
Projecting – Sketching – Shaping – Assembling
Original – Creative – Innovating – Groundbreaking
Novel – Imaginative – Inventive – Progressing – Dreaming
Envisaging – Planning – Visionary – Sculpting – Conceiving
Constructing – Construction – Sketching – Drawing
Outlining – Realising – Developing – Project – Thinking of
Brainstorming – Generating – Coming up with – Creativity
Prototype – Fanciful – Original – Arty – New – Fertile
Refined – Unexpected – Remarkable – Surprising
Gob smacking – Architect – Construction site – Breeding
Breeding ground – Striking – Grotesque – Amazing
Incubator

Explorer

Route – Discovering – Exploring – Guide – Journey – Travel
Companion – Borders – Horizon – World – Exploration
Terrain – Uncharted – Curious – New – Planet
Voyage of discovery – Jungle – Landscape – Trip
Trek – Tour – Unbeaten paths – Hike – On the way
Destination – Stop Stage – Further – Far – Station – Space
Extraterrestrial – Expedition – Sea – Stars – Moon – Desert
Mountains – On the road – Street – Road – Attraction
Area – Explorer – Adventure – Halt – Tourist – Experience
Wilderness – Excursion – Outing – Sightseeing – Track
Direction – Course – Compass – Transport – Transportation
Travelling – Solar system – Search – Columbus
Nova Zembla – Cape – Path – Lane – Finding out
Exposing – Experiencing – Keeping on track – Navigating
Navigation – Novel – Unheard of – Guiding – Shed
Warding – Turning – Sailing

Outlaw

Different – Revolution – Radical – Disruptive – F*ck it
Piss off – Bugger off – Against – Anti – New – Innovative
Reinvented – Spectacular – Dare – Courage – Courageous
Total – Fight – Be ahead – Different direction – Quicker
Better – Do you dare? – Frontrunners – Rioter – Uprising
Rebellion – Breaking the rules – Out of the box
Creativity Works! – Cannibal – Rebels – Novel – Status quo
Paradigm shift – Unusual – Different – Chaos
We'd like to see it different – But why? – Why…?
Imagine that – That is not necessary – Why would you?

15

Groundbreaking – Messed up – What if…? – Drastic
Extreme – Completely – Extremely – Radical – Protest
Recalcitrant – Opposition – Unruly – Battle – Friction
Struggle – Attack – Collision – Conflict – Alternative
Contrary – Stubborn – Rebellious – Subversive
Petulant – Riots – Mutiny

Have you made your choices? Great. Now you need to look at what this means in practical terms. Let's write a piece. We've developed a short, neutral example that you can rewrite in your own vocabulary and your own tone of voice.

Thanks for your order. Your order has been placed and is currently being processed. You will receive an email with the details of your order.

Is that all? Yes, that's all. You will be surprised how it can work out if you rewrite it with the above in mind. For example: informal, youthful, enthusiastic and archetype Jester.

Great! Your order has been received, Let's get this party started! Our people are running like crazy up and down our storage room to wrap up your order festively. Check your inbox because we've sent you an email with all the details and stuff. Thumbs up!

For example, formal, serious, mature and archetype Ruler.

Congratulations on your choice for top quality. Your order is exclusively being checked and carried out for you with the greatest accuracy. An email with a complete overview of your order will be sent to you.

Or: mature, with warmth and humour. Archetype Lover.

How wonderful that you share our passion. We've received your order and are processing it with love. Our love letter with all the details on our relationship will be sent to your email address. We're both heading for a great future.

THE MESSAGE OF MY BRAND

Rewrite the message below in the tone of voice of your brand. Don't forget to use your answers to the five questions and the word inspiration list.

Thanks for your order. Your order has been placed and is currently being processed. You will receive an email with the details of your order.

And now you!
...

WRITE
YOUR SLOGAN

Go on. We're on to a new way of tricking the Black Box; thinking of a sentence that gets the mind focused. A slogan. A payoff. A motto. All flashy jargon that boils down to the same thing: a nice line of text that tells what your brand wants to convey in an attractive way.

Well, you've known what your brand represented since you made your onliness statement. So now the challenge is to vocalise this core promise in such a way that it sounds good and sticks. And that it doesn't get on people's nerves after they've heard it ten times. You need to get your promise down on paper in a creative way that's short and snappy.

Making a slogan is playing with language. This means you can tap into the toolkit used by poets. Alliteration, for example, is a powerful tool. Take a look at the use of the F and the B in this slogan by Landrover: **The best four by four by far**. Rhyming vowels also produces good results: **The best a man can get**. Well done by Gillette. Or how about the power of repetition? **The few. The proud. The marines.** With such repetition an alliteration is naturally born. Wait, real pros combine everything they can: vowel rhyme, repetition and sound rhyme... **Plop, plop, fizz, fizz, what a relief it is**. You could try such a painkiller if thinking about a slogan gives you a headache.

What also works well is a slogan that can be interpreted in multiple ways. A sentence that can mean multiple things evokes excitement. It stimulates the brain. **Nothing runs like a deere** by John Deere is a good example. Or how about **Connecting people** conceived by Nokia, a brand that is pretty much defunct nowadays. Nothing to do with their slogan though.

Humour? Fine! Especially if your archetype is the Jester. But, as we've said before, don't be too silly. A slogan should last for a while. At least a year or five. And hopefully much longer.

The process is roughly the same as when thinking of a name. You start off by making a long list and cross things out until you've only got one left. Make sure that you schedule a couple of days for it. First take a good look at your onliness statement and then play around with words and sentences. It really is a matter of chewing and ruminating. The danger is that you will want to tell too much. This will lead to a slogan that's too long. You really have to get down to the core. You will see that if you're blessed with a feeling for language and you've completed the previous steps properly, you'll be fine.

Once you've got your slogan, test it out. Check if it has the intended effect on your target group. And check if someone didn't by chance come up with the same slogan ten years ago. This can prevent a lot of friction.

MY LIST OF SLOGANS

Write down your list of slogans and mark the definitive one!

...

...

...

...

...

...

...

...

...

...

16

WRITE THE
SHORT STORY

DNA, character, name, symbol, slogan, it's been quite a journey. Your newborn brand is practically up on its feet. After reading this book and completing the various filling out exercises, you've probably become even prouder. And so you should be. You've put a lot of time and energy into it and it has paid off. Now it's almost time to introduce your brand to others.

You can do this through numerous channels. Websites, presentations, brochures, social media strategies...There are many ways into the Black Box. We could attempt going over all of them here, but then the book will get thicker than our publisher would like. We do, however, think there is a way we can help you.

Whichever path you choose, you must be able to speak about your brand in a super clear and powerful way. You will need a convincing story. A story that expresses everything you've done so far. A story that gains its full potential in the Black Box. We're going to help you put this story together. We will start out small and will develop it later. We will progress from an ultra-short story, that you could tell whilst enjoying a beer at the bar, to a super-slick pitch in the last step. If you've nailed both, we think you'll also be able to tell your story through all other channels. Let's start with the ultra-short story.

A clear brand can be explained in just a couple of sentences. Together these sentences form a story that you'd want to tell at a networking event or in the corridors of a congress. But in your direct network, an ultra-short story is handy too. You get your family, friends, colleagues, acquaintances and random passers-by on board through your ultra-short story.

The ultra-short story is so important because it can be passed on. It's the contacts of your family, friends, colleagues and acquaintances who are interesting. And that is due to the fact that they form large numbers. Imagine you have a hundred acquaintances. If they all have a hundred acquaintances too, then you suddenly have a potential reach of 10,000 people. A part of them could well be in your target group.

That is if you ignore the fact that a part of these networks will overlap. In any case, this is exactly the principle that the success of LinkedIn is based on. These 10,000 people are all pretty sensitive to the info they get from their network. So if your network contacts pass the message on to their own networks in the pub, at the gym, or at their work, you've really hit the jackpot.

17

In other words, the ultra-short story is there to be passed on. This means that you need to work it out first and then be able to ad-lib it.

And no, this isn't easy. You will have to sit with it for a little bit. But hey, we haven't created space for filling out exercises in our book for nothing. So take a look at them again. Slogan, archetype, core values, the whole damn lot. But most of all: your onliness statement, as this will really reflect the core of your brand. From all this information you will distill three to four loosely formulated sentences that really show what your brand represents.

For an architect who once had the idea of specialising in building or renovating dental practices and GP surgeries, this could for example work out this way. This company would be very happy if you tell the story below to a friend or a colleague.

Building or renovating in the health sector means creating a place where professionals can work together comfortably every day. And where clients can feel good. Achieving this is specialist work, where it's easy to make a mistake which is difficult to rectify. If you're up against something like that, don't do your head in, but call XXX. They will understand where you're heading and really work together with you, are trustworthy and will look after your project from A to Z, which will lead to a smartly designed result that will give you years of pleasure.

Or a university of applied sciences that had
the idea to transform itself into a networking
organisation.

> *If you really want to do something with marketing or*
> *communication, you should take a look in Tilburg.*
> *At XXX Institute of Marketing and Communication*
> *they've got all the knowledge in-house. All degrees*
> *come with their own specialism, specifically sport and*
> *internationally oriented. And if one can't help you, the*
> *other can. They have strong networks in which they can*
> *easily find each other. A lot of interesting openings to do*
> *great things together. Future-oriented too. And focused*
> *on concrete results.*

MY SHORT STORY

Write down the short story of your brand.

...

DESIGN THE
WINNING PITCH

Did your ultra-short story work out? Then we'd like to take you to the last step. We're advancing from the ultra-short story to the next challenge. We're taking you into the world of professional pitching. If you can do this, you can probably do anything. It's the last step in our parenting trajectory to help you launch your newborn brand into the world and let it grow big. We've done this rather comprehensively, so take out what's relevant and necessary for you at this moment.

Maybe it's a good idea to explain here what exactly we have in mind when we speak of a professional pitch. It seems like there are quite a few people around that think a pitch always takes place in an elevator. But, we're not talking about the so-called elevator pitch here, whereby you tell your story in less than a minute. If it does happen that you bump into your target group in the elevator, the ultra-short story can do it's trick.

We're thinking of a setting, where professionals listen to your presentation of your newborn brand and its product or service. If these professionals are triggered enough in their Black Box, they'll be prepared to act. They will buy your product, fund

163

18

your newborn brand or introduce you to their network.

Once you've nailed the basis of your pitch, you can keep tailoring it to the audience that you have in front of you, to tell them all about your newborn brand, without being perceived as boring or irrelevant.

You may think that a good brand will just sell itself on that pitching stage. Unfortunately, this is not the case. We've organized enough pitching events to know how it really works. Too often a mediocre idea beats a good idea. Do you want to know why? It's simply 'sold' to people better. A lot more time and attention has been put into creating a good, convincing pitch. Not the idea, but the story that's told with it, is better. You can disagree, but it's the hard truth.

People, which also means the people who listen to ideas, are everything but rational and objective. They're easily manipulated. If you really want your newborn brand to become a winner, you need to make use of this. With the right preparation, you can create a pitch that matters and really touches the heart. If you don't do it and somebody else does, you won't stand a chance.

You can deliver a good pitch with a good, thorough preparation. Choose what's relevant for you at this particular moment. The choice is yours. And yes, if you have completed the previous 17 steps it will make things much easier for you.

Prepare

Start off by deciding what exactly you want to achieve with this pitch. Do you want to inform your audience about your newborn brand? Do you want to receive feedback on your product or services? Do you want to transmit your enthusiasm about your brand to others so they get involved? Or maybe you'd rather convince your audience to invest money in your brand and its product or service? If you don't know yourself what you want to achieve, how should your audience know what they're supposed to do? So take the time to focus on what your goal is. What behaviour of your audience are you aiming at? Then you can design your pitch in such a way that you will succeed.

Who are you pitching for? It's important beforehand to really identify with the audience of your pitch. They can be very diverse of course. Are you pitching for investors, lecturers, employees, the managing board, management team, customers, colleagues or a jury? And, how many of them are there? Are they male, female or mixed? Can you estimate their ages? What is the background of your audience? What type of personalities are they? Are they technical, commercial or creative people? Maybe you don't

18

know all the details, but the more you find out, the better you can prepare your pitch.

Subsequently you check where your pitch will be held. Is it a large room or a small room? A cold, gray, modern room, with a lot of natural light or no windows at all? Are you pitching in a space where multiple pitches are being held, such as a large exhibition space? Are you on a stage or on the same level as your audience? Is there competition? Find out if the area around you is quiet or if there's other noise. So reflect on the location where your pitch is being held. The more you find out, the better you can prepare and minimize possible distractions.

Are you standing up and is your audience seated? Or are you both sitting or standing up? Is there a (jury)table behind which your audience is seated? How formal is the setting? Are people walking around or are they centered around you? And what will you wear?

Find out how much time you've got for your pitch. Have you been given a timeslot with an exact number of minutes? Can you take as much time as you want? Will you get cut off after x minutes? How long do you think it should take? Will they signal to you when you've just got one minute left? Lastly, it's handy to assess what you need for your pitch or what's available. Is there a microphone? If so, what type of microphone? Is it hand held or a clip-on microphone that allows you to walk around? Do you need a laptop for your pitch? Can you connect it to a power supply? If you need a beamer, what type? Is your laptop compatible with the beamer? Make sure you've got the right adapter. Can you test everything beforehand to check it's all working? If you have a supporting presentation on your screen, make sure you don't have much text, use images.

Wow. A lot of preparation. Of course, you won't have the answers to all these questions. It doesn't matter. But the more information you've got, the better your preparation will be. And, the better your preparation, the more chance for success for you!

Are you ready to move on to the content? Let's develop your story the perfect way.

Execute

Your pitch starts here. It's important to immediately grab your audience's attention. You can choose from three different options. You can also combine two or even three of these options.

First option. Start with a short personal story. Preferably this story has a strong emotional component relating to your newborn brand. Try and keep it short and focused in order to touch

18

the right string with your audience. Ensure that your story stays compact. Too short is no good, but neither is too long.

Second option. Start with a significant statistic. People react strongly to this. It motivates them to ask themselves questions or form an opinion. Can you find a statistic that triggers your audience? One that is related to your brand of course. A triggering, purely random statistic for a start up with a bright new product to lock your front door could be: the average burglary takes less than 30 seconds. Yes, 30 seconds only...

Third option. Start with a stimulating question for your audience. A question makes sure you get people's attention. Your audience is immediately being activated, seeing as they have to think of an answer. Think carefully about your question, because this option can be a risky one. What will you do if you don't get any response? Or what if the answer to your question doesn't suit you? Posing a question means that you've given up control for the next ten or twenty seconds. If you're in doubt whether you'll be able to take back control easily, then it might be better not to do it after all.

A question can start with: are you also struggling with...? Who knows someone that...? A closed question ensures that you have more control as it is usually only answered with a yes or no.

Probably you now have the attention of your audience. Let's move on.

Your brand helps a specific group of people, your target group, to solve a problem or challenge. So zoom in on what they're running up against. What is the problem? Or what are the target group's challenges? What are the pains of your target group? Which emotions come to the surface in your target group with regard to the problem or challenge? And, importantly, who exactly are your target group? Or do you have more than one? Paint a clear picture of your target group and give them a face. Make it small and personal.

Subsequently, zoom out a bit. Who else is experiencing the problem your target group is struggling with? And what consequences does that have now? And in the near future? In other words, you paint a comprehensive picture of the problem at hand and the challenges that your newborn brand can fix.

So far, we have only talked about people with their problems. But, you could also have a very good, fun solution for a simple problem. This will make your pitch a lot lighter. Tailor the tone to your brand and your solution. At this moment, you've landed at an interesting point in your pitch. After involving your audience and explanation of the problems surrounding your target group and more, you now turn to your solution. You've

18

indicated what the status quo is and now you take a step towards the future you see ahead of you. You state that you believe that things don't need to be this way and that there's a solution to your target group's problem or challenge. Using the words "I am convinced that" or "I believe that"... usually works a treat. It will seem like your audience immediately asks themselves if they share your conviction. In order to answer this question for themselves, they will want to carry on listening to what you have to say.

Finally, now your solution can appear. You start off with the name of your brand. You could show a logo if you've already got one. You use colours that suit your brand and of course the idea itself. It can be physical but of course digital too. After that you take your audience on board with your idea and your brand. You explain it to them. You zoom in on the pros and cons and which problems or challenges it will eliminate for your target group. Try to include the functional as well as emotional aspects.

By nature people have all sorts of reservations. They can't help it. It's something from our past. That's why you should zoom in on possible reservations people could have about your idea. You then show your audience the solution you have in mind. You show them some realism, in fact. If your audience has already started to get excited about your newborn brand, then they'll soon ask about the costs. During this phase of your pitch you zoom in on the different aspects of the investment in your brand. Be aware that different target groups will need different information here. Where a potential customer will just need a purchase price, an investor will be curious how much money and how many hours you need to create your brand and what the business model is. He will also be longing for information on the know-how that is required. And which technology you depend on. Outline a clear plan of how you think you can achieve this and who you need for which part.

The end of your pitch is in sight. You can conclude your pitch in roughly two different ways. Of course, you can combine them again. See what feels right for you.

First option. Conclude with a short summary. Briefly zoom in on the highlights, what you want to achieve and finish with your slogan and/or call to action.

Second option. Finish off by sketching the future horizon. If your brand becomes a success, what else is possible in the near future? Give your audience a brief glimpse into the future. Keep it realistic though and don't get started on world peace etcetera. End with your slogan and a call to action. For this, take another look back at what exactly you wanted to achieve.

18

Afterparty

A pitch is usually followed by a round of questions. Of course, there will always be surprising questions, but with a bit of preparation, you can also take this last hurdle with a smile. You can sit down beforehand and think up some questions your audience could ask. These can be all sorts of questions. It really depends on who your audience is. Commercial people ask different questions than technical people. And technical people ask different questions than creative people.

Obvious questions could be: what was your target group's feedback on your idea? How much money do you think you will make in the first year or first three years? What really sets your product or service apart from what's already out there? What are your solution's weak aspects?

Write down as many questions as possible that you can think of. And answer them. This really ensures that you can stand on your two feet at the afterparty and that your pitch is different from others.

That's right, an outstanding pitch requires a lot of work. Believe us, it's worth it.

CONGRATULATIONS
YOU JUST DID IT

We started this book with congratulations. Here we do it again. First we congratulated you with your idea, now we congratulate you with your fully-grown brand!

You've done some pretty hard work during the previous 18 steps. All the effort you put into it will now really pay off. Good job!

Are you finished now? No, of course not. New fun starts right here. Your brand is, let's put it this way, an adolescent now, ready to go into the tough outside world and enter into grown up friendships.

At this moment you have a clear picture of what your newborn brand offers and to whom. You gave it character. You have established the most important values. And by formulating your onliness statement you provided focus. You have your own colours, a shiny name, even a matching vocabulary and a great story.

On page 15, we kindly asked you to wait to go wild on all sorts of communication around your idea. Finally, the time is right for you to let yourself be seen and heard.

a

Keep focus on your target group, set your objectives, choose a strategy and pick your communication channels.

You're ready for it. Let's party in the Black Box.

We're sure you won't f*ck it up. ☺

Good luck!

WE JUST WANT
TO SAY THANK YOU

Well, we feel it's a great honour that you've got this far. This feels satisfying and gives us energy to start working on a new idea. Maybe even a new book, who knows? Before that happens, we'd like to thank a couple of people. Our thanks go out to:

You as our reader. You were the best reader ever. If you ever happen to bump into us and you've got this book with you, we'd love to scribble this in your book. With a real pen and a proper signature.

Everyone who's given us feedback in the development phase of this book. Without your help it would have never turned out this way. If it's not good enough, it kind of is your fault, but in any case thanks a lot!

Our girlfriends. Good that you left us to our devices and that you granted us all the time needed to write a book and put up with the strange behaviour that comes with it. Maybe you too found it nice and quiet that we were busy with something else. But thanks, anyway.

e

Our parents. Once we were babies too. Apparently, you didn't need this parenting book to get to an acceptable result. You've done a great job. We reap the benefits every day.

Each other. Again, we didn't really argue and we laughed a lot. Let's keep it that way.

And last but not least we would like to say sorry to everyone who feels insulted or hurt by this book. Seems unlikely but even so. Before you know it, we are entangled in legal proceedings. Which we don't feel like.

A unique time is drawing to a close. We've enjoyed this adventure.

Enjoyable, that's what it was. Goodbye!

Joris & Coen